CHOOSING AN OFFSHORE:
Cybertax in the New Millennium

MICHAEL H. GROSH

WITH ERIC R. GREIF

ORChard Hill Press
Calgary and Lancaster

Copyright © Michael H. Grosh 2000

Published by Orchard Hill Press
Box 37, Fenton Street, Lancaster, Lancashire LA1 1WZ England
and 32011 Bankview RPO, Calgary, Alberta T2T 5X6 Canada
www.orchardhillpress.com

Canadian Cataloguing in Publication Data

Grosh, Michael H. & Greif, Eric R.

Choosing an offshore: cybertax in the new millennium

Includes bibliographical references and index.
ISBN 0-9686846-0-2

British Library Cataloguing-in-Publication

A catalogue record for this book is available from the British Library

Typeset in Los Angeles by Moni Scaria
Printed in New York City by Phoenix Color
Cover Photo by Michael Grosh
Designed and Edited by Eric Greif

Information on International Consultants Enterprises
can be found at www.offshoretaxation.com

ACKNOWLEDGEMENTS

To my Editor, Colleague, Friend and "adopted Baby Brother", Eric Greif, also known as "Little ICE". Eric's inspiration and courage under adverse health and other conditions was a true inspiration that kept me going on this project. To Deborah Kay for her contributions to the Trust section and for constantly giving me enough aggravation to spur my creative juices.

Other thanks to Rick and Bonnie Pollick and their boys, for accepting a virtual stranger into their lives and putting up with me through thick and thin. To Cindy Staniloff, for making me smile and see things from another perspective, and to the rest of my family back in Toronto, and all the professionals throughout the world who took the time to talk to me and helped to develop my ideas.

This Book is Dedicated to My Dad,

Abraham Jacob Grosh,

who brought happiness to many and will sorely be missed.

TABLE OF CONTENTS

INTRODUCTION

Business is a beast whose thirst is only quenched by success and wealth. Likewise, a hard worker also measures his or her success by the ability to save for the future. The objective of this book is to reveal a set of programs that will assist major businesses, professionals and individuals in making a choice of international tax haven, effectively and efficiently. This in-depth analysis will attempt to provide a structured data bank for use by the non-specialist adviser on offshore vehicles, as well as for the specialist. It is for the business owner trying to maximise the worth of the company. It is for the person who has been working abroad and needs assistance with the status of their earnings. It is for the individual seeking tax avoidance in a legal manner. It introduces concepts, explains the important aspects of taxation internationally, and gives insight into many international offshore locations.

The systems that are exposed by Dr. Grosh throughout this book have come from years of research, as a Chartered Accountant, a Ph.D. in International Tax, and as a tax lawyer. Theories are developed in the latter part of the book utilising the computer in analysing complex situations. Large amounts of relevant data, not easily accessible in the past, are exposed here. With the increased availability of such information, proper planning can be made by the businesses involved, or for the individual wage earner.

To develop such a system, various questions must be asked regarding offshore tax havens:

1. What are the major uses of the offshore locations?
2. What factors must be considered in choosing the most appropriate offshore arrangement for the client's circumstances?
3. What weight must be given to each factor?
4. Are consultants consistent in their choices of offshore locations?

Dr. Grosh effectively answers the questions, and provides solutions. He offers concise illustrations, charts, test problems, check lists and data. It has been my honour to edit and make occasional additions to this work. This book is the tool of choice for the professional or the interested consumer seeking to find the proper offshore.

So, start the cybertax trip from the ice...to the paradise.

ERIC R GREIF, B.A., LL.B., LL.M., Iredell Fellow in Law
Member of the Canadian Bar Association (Alberta Branch)
and the International Law Association (British Branch)

CHAPTER 1
CONSIDERING THE
OFFSHORE TAX HAVEN

The reduction of tax provides more capital for the operation of businesses. One way of approaching it is appreciating that taxes dispose of financial resources that could normally be used in the business; a reduction in tax would free such resources. The freedom of resources provides more funds to expand the business and therefore can lead to an increase in employment. This increase in employment could in turn provide more tax revenue to the home country through personal taxation. Thus, the use of tax havens in reducing taxation to a business can indirectly have a positive effect on an economy.

The use of several tax havens provides flexibility within the world financial system. It allows further protection of confidentiality and anonymity through the separation of functions and other barriers. These are presented by the insertion of political barriers to an outside regulatory body that is making an attempt at tracing an entity.

One problem that exists is the question of how long the major powers will allow the mechanisms of tax havens to operate. Further questions abound such as how much secrecy is actually involved in international tax havens, as well as how fine should the line be drawn between tax evasion and tax avoidance. These and other problems are dealt with in this book. The position on an offshore location in relation to the international business community is becoming more and more important. More and more governments are creating special task forces to look into the problem of potential tax revenue being moved from the home country to one of these offshore locations. Anti-avoidance measures are being introduced by the major powers to stop the use of offshore locations. As a result, offshore locations and vehicles are constantly being set up and broken down. This imposes a burden on the taxpayer to insure the proper professional advice is obtained to adequately consider the changes in local and domestic laws.

Some offshore locations have proven very successful, whereas others have had difficulty in establishing themselves in the world market. The reason for this occurrence is that tax havens are not merely a vehicle for the reduction of tax, but they also provide for ease of international trade. People of wealth are looking to their use in an attempt to retain more of the profits they have been able to make. With burgeoning interest in offshore locations, there is a large demand created for expert professional advice on the choice of offshore locations, their use, and how close the user wants the offshore to be located from their home country.

Offshore taxation professionals are masters of a specific service, and they possess knowledge and expertise not normally obtained by a standard tax consultant. This area of specialisation requires an in-depth knowledge and understanding of the relationship between local and domestic laws on the one hand, and the laws of the offshore location on the other. The customary tax lawyer or tax accountant traditionally has a limited knowledge of offshore locations and would normally advise their clients that such locations and vehicles of use would be considered as evasion. The facts reveal this to be spurious. It is the general lack of knowledge of offshore use by practitioners that leads instances to such overly cautious and misleading advice.

The use of offshore locations is similar to utilising any loophole in a country's tax system to derive a benefit and to reduce tax burden. For domestic taxation, the use of a loophole requires a change in the tax law to render the set-up illegal. Similarly, if properly set-up, an offshore vehicle would require a change in the local law to make it ineffective. In this way the two are similar in nature and cannot be considered evasion.

When evaluating offshore locations, other conditions need to be considered. Some of these are:

1. Political considerations
2. Financial
3. Behavioural aspects and communication
4. Reliability and Stability.

Political Considerations

In evaluating the feasibility of an offshore location, consideration should be given to whether or not the home country has good relations with the offshore location. If good relations do not exist, the home country might decide to bar any activity involving that country. Most tax departments have the ability to make this decision as a result of a special section in their local tax legislation giving them to power to exercise discretion whether or not a transaction is proper or merely an attempt to avoid tax.

Any dealings with offshore locations usually have triggered negative reactions from local tax departments. This must be viewed as a given reality in all situations. As such, to avoid complications and undue harassment by taxation officials and other regulatory bodies and their representatives, it is best to have the utmost in confidentiality and anonymity in all such dealings. Other considerations include whether the offshore location requires aid from the home country. How dependent is the offshore location on its tax-free status? Whether or not their status as a low tax, offshore location produces minor or major revenues for the offshore country is a question of prime importance. If the country's tax haven status produces only a minor amount of its revenue, the slightest pressure from a major power could result in the state changing their law.

Financial

What is the major financial use of an offshore location? Is it to avoid tax or are there other valid reasons? Many entities use off-shore tax havens simply to avoid taxation, and this is a given reality, but it is clearly not the only reason. To avoid tax, there are quite a few schemes that have been devised. Although one can obtain a list of such methods, it is always best to consult a professional to insure the method is properly set-up and it is applicable in the situation concerned. Most situations require a specialised scheme involving several countries, other tax laws and an intermingling of tax treaties. This is not to suggest that every scheme is unique. As a matter of fact, most have certain general characteristics, with only minor modifications required to fit a unique situation. For many situations the amount of money paid for professional advice is minor compared to the level of savings and term of use.

Many companies depend on the movement of funds, controls on the way international business is conducted, and other factors of a similar nature. This qualifies as being a non- tax financial reason for the use of offshore locations. Another incentive is the protection of assets from other third parties, including governments, creditors, spouses, bankruptcy, litigation and other potential claims on assets.

Behavioural Aspects and Communication

Behavioural aspects must also be considered in choosing an offshore country. Do the people of that country accept and welcome these foreigners with assets into their country to do business? Are they resentful of the wealth the foreigners' possess or the power and control that they exert? Are they willing to work efficiently? How does the general public of the home country - for example the United States - feel about the person or business avoiding taxation? If there is resentment, is there a positive public movement towards stopping the use of offshores? In the matter of communication, does the offshore country offer the international company easy access so that it may function properly in accordance with its needs for international trade and general business?

As a general piece of advice, distance as well as speed are major factors for consideration of an offshore location. The speed of action required to perform basic administrative functions is very important. For example, if it takes three weeks for one simple order to be implemented, consideration must be given to using that country on a limited basis. However, It is also worthwhile to note that the length of time to do the initial incorporation is not necessarily a guideline for performing other functions. The incorporation of a company, or establishment of a Trust, or a combination of both, usually require government registration which tends to be much slower than the speed of executing orders given to a private institution such as a bank.

Reliability and Stability

Can the government in the offshore country be relied upon to uphold their word of assurance? Is written assurance enough to provide the user the required comfort level.? One thing the user of an offshore country must consider, is whether or not the country is stable enough to be relied upon. If there is internal strife, a new ruling revolutionary power would disregard all commitments made by their

predecessors and seize all assets. It is essential that assets be controlled in such a way as to insure that they are moved to a location
that is secure.

Work On Offshore Locations

International law specifically relating to offshore locations is
subject to many forms of constructive criticism by practical experts.
Such criticisms are welcomed, as they serve to expand the scope of
research in the area. There is very little research done on the benefits
of offshore locations. This is apparently due to the lack of understanding of local researchers and a general reluctance in considering
factors on a global basis. On an international scale, a great deal of
patience is necessary, as the complications are numerous. As more
countries are considered, in conjunction with their internal legislation
regarding foreign operations, a complex system results that is constantly changing. To study such a large-scale system would require a
great deal of financing and international co-operation. As yet, such
resources are not available due to the inherent mistrust of countries
with their neighbours. This lack of research in some instances is to the
advantage of those who use offshore locations, as it is a hindrance to
taxation authorities; it is difficult for cohesion and solidarity in formu-
lating customary rules to curb offshore benefits. The disadvantage of
such a lack of research for the person or business in need is that the
true benefits are not recognised and a beneficial system will not be
developed for that client. International tax law is volatile in its changing nature and this requires the utmost care in order to conduct a
proper, efficient analysis. Expertise in all aspects of international law
is virtually impossible, therefore a consultant must choose a particular
sector as the object of their knowledge and abilities.

Most research on the topic of offshore tax havens has been restricted to only a few informed writers. Information about the laws of countries involved is fairly limited, as writers for the most part have been interested in dealing with persons who represent potential business for themselves. The emphasis of many tax experts is on selling a particular offshore market, without adequate analysis of the overall offshore possibilities, thus greatly diminishing information available for clients so vital in choosing the proper offshore location. Their general style of discussion involves statements of a few relationships about offshore locations, followed by a more detailed analysis on the specific country.

The main theme of this book is that an offshore decision making scheme should instead focus on the desired characteristics the particular client needs, then look at the elements required of an offshore, and finally to analyse the specific offshore locations. This gives the greatest flexibility.

CHAPTER 2
TOOLS OF THE TRADE

It is important to recognise that international taxation affects the countless thousands of individuals, corporations, and other entities that do business at, have assets in, or received income from a country other than their place of residence. The significance of such effects on the prosperity of nations and the maintenance of such wealth requires careful analysis of the offshore country. This chapter mainly concerns itself with identifying those concepts that are to be used for valuation of the basic tax haven scheme of operations. The principles underlying the idea of a tax haven can be quite subjective and complex. This chapter is designed to provide the reader with the basic interactive concepts that are combined to produce a true understanding of limitations, constraints and problems inherent in any type of complex tax haven operation. The use of these concepts in a Simulation Model (see Appendix) is not directly observable; they represent the underlying principles that are needed to value a tax haven and its use. Therefore, they have an indirect relevance to the formulation of the expert system and its implementation (the Simulation).

The definition of a tax haven is not as easily understood as one might expect, and indeed many experts have their own unique terminology to explain it. The separate definitions usually vary widely in their scope, therefore It is easier to facilitate one's own interpretation of those ideas for the process of showing the essentials of the concept.

The tax base is a concept used to value how a country will determine the allocation of relevant tax laws. That is, every country uses a particular basis for the assessment of tax. Since all countries have their own distinct notion on the definition of these bases, it is most relevant to recognise a few of these opinions on the subject. The reader need only understand differences in such definitions to truly visualise the complicated nature of international taxation and its contributing factors. To facilitate such knowledge, a brief description of these concepts is given for a few selected countries. Once the base for taxation is understood it is helpful to know how tax authorities formulate opinions on the legality of the tax scheme, this being the idea of *evasion vs. avoidance*. Tax authorities of the home country must decide whether transactions should be viewed as legal (avoidance), or illegal (evasion). Once this is determined, they decide what action to take. Since this study is based solely on the legal use of tax havens, the legality of any situation must be established before any type of analysis can proceed.

The characteristics that are used to evaluate whether a client should choose one tax haven over another is directly relevant to the decision-making process simulated in later chapters. One cannot choose among various tax haven countries without using a criterion for the choice. These characteristics are derived through a general consensus of experts in the field (a survey of experts was conducted).

The Tax Haven

The term tax haven is used to refer to a jurisdiction - a place:

1. where there are no relevant taxes;
2. where taxes are levied only on internal taxable events (or not at al), at low rates, and on profits from different sources; or
3. where special tax privileges are granted to certain types of taxable persons or events.

These special privileges may be given by the local internal tax system or could be derived as a result of domestic and treaty provisions used in combination. The above definition lays out the guidelines for the existence and function of a tax haven. True understanding of the tax haven concept requires further analysis of the inherent basis and goals.

Tax havens deal with the issue of paying as little taxes as possible. The term tax refers to income tax as well as other forms. Without getting into the sociological and modern cultural debate about supporting one's society, for the most part internationally businesses and individuals do not like paying taxes. This cauldron of players, namely taxpayers, accountants, lawyers, consultants and revenue officials, are constantly engaged in the never-ending battle between taxation of wealth on the one hand, and preserving financial holdings through the reduction of taxation the public is obliged to pay on the other.

Why do businesses and individuals object to paying tax? Perhaps the best answer to this question is that the public is far removed from the operation of government spending. The public in many instances cannot see directly how taxes are being spent, or they object to misspending or large civil bureaucracies. Besides this, it appears mankind has a built-in desire to ensure that all expenditures parted with are used to produce a worthwhile product. Is tax money truly spent by a government in a manner that benefits the public? In other words, businesses and persons with earning like to know the tax contributions are being used properly and efficiently. Many believe the cost of the state benefits that are provided are less than the value of the taxes that are paid. As such information will never be disclosed in its entirety, people will always feel it is their right to avoid paying taxes as much as possible. The popular perception is that every tax-payer has a legal right to decrease the amount of taxes they must pay, or completely avoid them, by any means that is allowable according to the written law. It is therefore the taxpaying business or individual's right to avoid paying taxes, as long as their attempt does not contra-vene the laws of the land.

A tax haven is a country that imposes little or no income tax and little or no death duty. Haven is a pleasant word, defined as being a place of protection, shelter and safety. When a person accumulates a fair sum of money through their own skill or luck they are constant-ly being harassed by those forces wishing to share in their good for-tune. Some of these factors are inflation, economic and political, the threat of expropriation, creditors and governments, to name a few. The world market also has an affect on the value of the taxpayer's home currency.

There are essential elements that make an offshore country desirable as a tax haven. Some of these factors are:

1. Favourable tax laws
2. Revenue safety
3. Political stability
4. Economic stability
5. Know-how
6. Tradition.

Favourable Tax Laws

Many countries possess favourable income tax laws, for both foreigners and residents. The main consideration is whether or not there exist any hidden taxes. A small island might have no income tax, yet the cost of the goods and services on the island could be quite outrageous. The total scheme must be viewed to ensure that those seeking a haven are not sacrificing one tax for another.

Revenue Safety

The laws of a tax haven may provide for little or no income tax, yet this benefit may strictly be a dilution. If that particular country has become especially popular with those seeking financial escape, or is suddenly the chic spot to go for the specific reason of evading taxation, transactions through that country could be labelled as illegal. All major economic powers have tax specialists and investigators in their government bodies who officially deal with the existence of such countries. Any transaction using these haven hot spots could be heavily investigated and potentially deemed a sham.

The assurance of favourable laws is also essential. Such assurances always have the drawback of being easily changed by new political parties gaining power. The only assurance of this type is the long tradition of integrity exercised by that particular country. Canada and the United States have implemented many changes in their tax legislation to try and prevent tax haven activities. However, the limit to such actions is the fact that they also want to encourage international trade in recognition of the movement toward a global economy.

Political and Economic Stability

A newly developing country or one that has a history of political creates an unwarranted risk for tax travellers looking to use offshore countries. Since the laws can be changed as fast as they are created, and assets can also be seized at random, it is advisable to completely avoid any tax haven that has a hint of instability. Tax savings alone cannot be the only consideration for choosing a sanctuary, as economic stability in that haven country is equally important. A country with questionable economic policies, or a history of instability, will be subject to influences for change internally and externally. Such influences breed erratic shifts and possible disaster to tax travellers.

Certain tests are suggested for the further testing of a potential haven's stability:

- bank privacy
- lack of government intervention
- democratic country with political stability
- conservative banking laws
- a strong backing for its currency
- international status
- freedom of currency movement
- characteristics of the people
- international banks
- qualified local professional

The above are but a few of the many areas that need to be investigated.

Know-how

Perhaps the least used yet most important tool is the existence of internal knowledge. No matter how favourable laws can be, there must be people to exercise the laws as well as run the businesses. When looking to some of the newest tax havens, one must be assured that there is an acceptable level of sophistication in the institutions and people involved to insure that instructions and transactions can be probably executed. This conservative approach insures that business can be run relatively problem-free. It provides confidence as to the safety of assets, and any transactions involving those assets.

Tradition

Understanding the past leads to confidence in future predictions. Predictive models use the past to predict the future. There's a great deal of emphasis that must be given to the history of a country for forecasting its future use. Therefore, ideals like the standards of decency, revolutionary spirit, a political upheaval, prosperity and beliefs contribute to the good tradition of a country.

The liability for tax is dependent on certain so-called connecting links between the basis for taxation or the jurisdiction, and the taxpayer or taxable event. For individuals, the main links are residence, domicile and citizenship. For a company, they are management, and control, ownership and place of incorporation. Other links include the centre of economic interests as well as permanent establishment. At times, the residence of Trustees, and indeed even any affiliated persons, could be the determining connection to establish where income is taxed. For a Trust, basic law could dictate that the residence of the Trust is the residence of the Trustee. For a corporation, usually the location of mind and management of the company is considered. Also for a corporation, the residents of the directors could be relevant.

For a taxable event, the link is the deemed source. This is the source that has been established by legislation. This deemed source affects the liability to tax and the computation of the tax burden. The absence of any considerable world-wide communication and co-operation of fiscal systems (i.e. lack of co-operation among countries) produces the climate for the existence of tax havens.

Tax Base

The basis for taxation is an important consideration in determining how an offshore can be used in relation to the home country. Many countries impose tax on any income earned anywhere, based upon the residence of the taxpayer. Mere residence is not usually the sole criteria, especially for foreign source income. Usually, the permanent residence or domicile is taken into account. Escaping taxes in some cases can be as easy as changing the residence to a country with more favourable laws. Various countries possess differing opinions on the exact definition of the term *residence*. For a better understanding of the total concept of this term, situations are described for Austria, Denmark, France, Germany, Luxembourg, Switzerland and the United Kingdom. These countries are chosen because, from observing their interpretations, a good understanding of what is included in residency can be derived. One can see that these concepts are fairly similar in most countries.

Austria

In Austrian law, the term *Aufenthalt* (translates as "stay") is used as the closest to residence in characteristics. It is based purely on factual information and refers to a municipality as a territorial area. The term residence denotes the place in which a person is physically located. This can be permanent, temporary, voluntary, involuntary, internationally or by chance. Time is not a necessary condition. The term habitual residence is also used. It refers to a place in which a person is habitually located for considerably long periods. Continuous location is irrelevant and it must be a centre of person's activities, socially and economically. Permanent residence is the same as habitual residence.

Denmark

In Danish law, the term residence is established purely by interpretation. Usually it refers to a place where a person resides permanently, except for temporary absences for business, illness and other short-term periods. Under almost all circumstances a person's property where they are domiciled would be deemed their residence. The person's residence is recorded in a central registry, and as soon as the person resides in another location, the registry is informed and all documentation of residency changed.

France

In France, the general statutory provision does not exist governing residence as it does for domicile. In each case, provision has to be made as to its definition in a special text. The concept refers to an address, this being a place designated precisely enough to permit its determination. In clear language this means it must be clearly identifiable either physically or using some other means. It refers to a place where a person actually lives on a regular and habitual basis. The term habitual indicates where a person resides as a matter of habit. The definition of residence often coincides with the definition of domicile. In the case where the habitual residence is different than the domicile, it is considered a secondary establishment and is left to the courts to decide whether it is considered a residence.

Germany

In Germany, as in Austria, the law dictates the concept of residence in the expression *Aufenthalt,* or place of residence, common habitual residence and habitual place of residence. Exact definitions of these terms are not given, and they only refer to where a person actually dwells and is not merely a transient. Thus in Germany, it is usually in the courts where residence is determined. As in many countries, this is a common law approach where the government looks to the facts of the situation to determine where a person normally or habitually lives, and is not merely a transient.

Luxembourg

In Luxembourg, when dealing with civil procedure, the concept of residence is used as a substitute for domicile when a person's domicile is not known. It is important to understand that domicile is a legal concept that describes where a person is located. The law of domicile follows the principle that an individual can only have one domicile at any particular time. A person can only change from one domicile to another and they cannot give up one domicile without taking on another. Thus, domicile can only be exchanged it cannot be erased. The term residence is merely accepted as a material fact attaching to a person's physical presence in a place. In the courts, each case must be decided based on the facts. Usually, the courts look to domicile as a determining factor. The law in Luxembourg requires that such people are government employees, notaries and magistrate. The residence therefore refers to the actual abode where a person concerned performs their duties and where their activities and family are situated. The recognised definition for tax purposes refers to it as the place where the taxpayer resides in circumstances that indicate that his or her stay is not temporary. Any stay longer than six months renders a person liable to taxation as a resident (it is important to note that Canadian laws are similar to these, with the same basis for their determination).

Switzerland

In Swiss law, the concept of residence refers to the fact that the domicile of a person is at the place where they reside with the intention of settling. Thus, their law puts emphasis on intention as the key factor in determining whether a person is resident in the location or not. This place is considered the domicile if their previous domicile cannot be established. The Swiss utilise the definition in establishing that if the domicile cannot be determined, then they will use other means to ascertain where residency is. Residence is the place where a person is staying, as long as the stay is an extended one. Again, there is the common element in establishing residence quite close to the various countries mentioned.

United Kingdom

In England and Wales, the most commonly used terms are residence and ordinarily resident (a similar relationship is used in Canada and the United States, where ordinarily resident is similar to habitual resident). Residence has a variety of meanings that must be decided to fit the situation. It is normally considered the place where one resides, an abode or house (this can also include a rental accommodation, such as a hotel). This may also include a person's place of business. For income tax purposes, having a house in the United Kingdom and making occasional visits to that house, or living in a yacht anchored close to the shore, or even just making periodic visits to the United Kingdom for substantial periods (including staying in hotels or with friends) may, according to the circumstances, constitute residence and give rise to a liability for tax. Ordinarily resident refers to a particular habit of life. For a corporate body, this habit of life would be where central control and management is carried on. These laws apply to Scotland, as well as Canada, and in many instances to the United States.

In Austria, Denmark, Germany, Switzerland and the United Kingdom, aliens are not treated any differently from nationals with regard to residence. In France, the treatment is the same except for regulations regarding current control and investments. In Luxembourg, the courts have not decided whether an alien can have a domicile without proper authorisation.

The concept of residence is used to establish a link between a person and place. Certain rules concerning territorial jurisdiction are based on habitual residence, which is used in private international law. The concept takes into account most essential territorial conditions that allow the criterion of intention to become less important since it is very subjective. This term also solves the problem of the person who exists under legal guidelines as a stateless person.

It can be seen from the above analysis that intention is a very important consideration for residence. Yet, despite the important, it is very subjective in nature and revenue authorities as well as courts would prefer to narrow its use by establishing guidelines that are less subjective. The common interpretation among most countries (including the United States. and Canada) is that the facts of each situation will dictate the determination of residence. Although it appears that all these countries are similar in determination of their residence, since the decision ultimately is passed to the courts, the common law in each country is in fact different, and thus the facts that they look towards in making their determination greatly differ. As an overall guideline, one can look at where a person actually lives on a non-temporary basis.

Evasion vs. Avoidance

No matter what country is concerned, there's a fine line between tax avoidance and tax evasion which is not always made crystal clear. Many of the revenue authorities fail to distinguish between the two. Evasion has been spelled out as the commission or omission of attacks knowingly with intent to deceive so that the tax reported by the taxpayer is less than the tax payable under the law, or a conspiracy to commit such an offence. This may be accomplished by the deliberate omission of revenue, the fraudulent claiming of expenses or allowances and the deliberate misrepresentation, concealment or withholding of material facts.

In a mouthful, tax avoidance involves those cases where the taxpayer has apparently circumvented the law, without giving rise to a criminal offence by the use of the scheme, arrangement or device, often of complex nature, the main or sole purpose of which is to defer or completely avoid the tax payable under the law. Usually, a series of transactions is involved which do not truly reflect what is actually happening, and sometimes the avoidance is accomplished by shifting liability for tax to other taxpayers, not at arm's length, in whose hands the tax payable is reduced or eliminated.

It is very important that the distinction between tax evasion and tax avoidance is understood. Most people who criticise offshore locations feel that the use of tax havens is illegal and thus evasion. In reality, if the offshore vehicle were used properly, the home country law would need to be changed to prevent the vehicle from being used. As such, the use of an offshore vehicle done properly, with just advise, would be considered tax avoidance, and thus not illegal.

The term tax avoidance explains itself; it is without the criminal intention of evading taxation that comes with, as example, fraud. This term is quite neutral in its meaning because sometimes taxes are avoided through the use of legal measures and loopholes that happened to be against the spirit of the law, and in some cases the taxpayer may be deemed to have abused the law. Under these conditions, penal measures cannot be instituted and it is the lawgivers who must be relied upon to prevent the success of avoidance.

Clever taxpayers have been creative in their use of various tax acts to their own advantage, and to the displeasure of revenue authorities. One of the major techniques that have been employed by the courts in recent years, to prevent the use of such loopholes, has been the disallowance of so-called sham transactions. It is a very difficult proposition to separate real and sham transactions. The first consideration is what the real purpose is behind the transaction, not what the parties involved call it. More importantly, if two *bona fide* systems of transactions exist, one which is taxable under the statute while a second one is not taxable, the existence of the first system cannot make the second liable for tax. In permitting schemes to allow for reduction in tax, only those schemes have been allowed that the ruling judge feels have some other genuine business purpose. Thus, the courts have traditionally looked to the hypothetical business purpose of a transaction to justify its legality. For offshore vehicles using this type of approach, one would like to emphasise the non-tax reasons as the main purpose of structuring the transaction.

A Swiss Viewpoint

In Switzerland, violations of tax law are usually divided into five categories:

1. Deceit of tax by either simple tax evasion or qualified tax evasion (tax fraud);
2. Attempt to defeat tax;
3. Minor offences;
4. Violation of procedural duties by third persons;
5. Fiscal offences connected with Estate inventory.

Tax evasion is a result of three elements:

1. Failure to pay taxes or partial payment of tax;
2. Violation of the legal duty and responsibility of the taxpayer;
3. The taxpayers wilful intent to evade taxes or negligence;

Generally, tax evasion does not take place as long as the effective assessment is not contested and enforced. Evasion results when the taxpayer fails to file a return and therefore cannot be assessed. To the Swiss, tax fraud is a form of tax evasion in which the taxpayer deceives the tax authorities with false, forged, or incorrect documents. Tax fraud is considered a category of tax evasion subject to more severe penalties under most tax laws. An attempt at simple or qualified tax evasion is considered as an independent tax offence. It is considered successful when the assessment can no longer be changed through ordinary channels, that is, when it becomes incontestable and enforceable. A second category recognised by the Swiss is called the disobedience offence, or tax infraction. An offence of this category is committed when a taxpayer or third party is said to endanger the Estate inventory.

Penalties imposed for violation of taxes usually consist of money awards, and may be penal taxes or fines. A penal tax is used in cases of tax evasion or tax fraud, being the multiplier, or less frequently, a fraction of the under paid or jeopardised tax. In spite of a maximum and middle of the penal tax established by law, the actual amount of tax is fixed via tax authority. The fines are imposed for a minor infraction, violation of Estate inventory, and for offences committed by persons not responsible for the payment of taxes (people who helped with the offence, accessories to the offence, or the legal representative of the taxpayer). In the case of fraud, fines are imposed in addition to tax penalties. The maximum amount is provided for by law, as written in the legislation. The Swiss consider international tax avoidance as a reduction of tax liability through the movement or non-movement of persons or funds across tax boundaries by legal methods. It can be seen that the Swiss view the avoidance of taxes as a right of the individual or corporation and only in cases similar to fraud do they have an objection.

Other wealthy countries have a different viewpoint on the topic of evasion vs. avoidance, locally and internationally.

The Netherlands

In the Dutch tax laws and treaties, there is more recognition given to avoidance for individuals than businesses. In the Netherlands, the general approach taken derives its importance from the exact wording of the law, rather than the spirit or intent of the law.

In many cases the spirit of the law is almost of equal importance and many a case has been decided with the intention of producing an equal and reasonable solution. The charge of taxes is therefore based strictly on the written law as specified in legislation. The law is seldom seen as being abstract and short, favouring the general case rather than the specific. For example, the law uses economic value as a basis for valuation. This is a very broad and general valuation method. Another aspect is a strict reliance of the tax authorities on the certification by accountants.

The Dutch believe that every taxpayer can arrange their affairs in the cheapest way. Thus, they do believe that a person is allowed to arrange their affairs in such a way as to pay a minimum of tax. As has been proven by the common law, the Dutch believe that the pursuit of tax saving is a valid reason for arranging affairs into a particular way. A Dutch citizen using a tax haven does not have to come out with another reason for justifying the use of the offshore. The reduction of taxes is a sufficient reason. The only time that this rule can be disregarded is when the transaction is deemed to contravene the purpose of that particular law in question.

The benefit of such a regime to, for example, someone from the United States or Canada, is that it is beneficial to use a screen company in the Netherlands as an intervening entity. Since Dutch tax rates are not dissimilar from those in the United States, their use by an American would not be viewed by the Internal Revenue Service as a vehicle to reduce taxes. Therefore, the use of a tax haven by the Dutch intermediary would only be scrutinised by the Dutch authorities. The Dutch authorities, of course, believe in tax reduction as a proper reason for structuring a transaction. In this way a proper vehicle can be put togetherwith minimal obstruction by revenue authorities in the various home countries.

United Kingdom

Like most of the European countries, the United Kingdom taxes a resident on their world-wide income and non-residents on their UK source income. This general law is subject to specific laws or treaties that take into account specific cases and override the general law. The UK uses the remittance basis for individuals. This basis catches any enjoyment of income in United Kingdom by residence, whether the money was made domestically or abroad. Thus residence is the key in the UK. This is similar to the laws of Canada, and the laws of the United States base a similar rule on citizenship. A gift of such income loses its quality as income and may be paid by the individual without tax liability. There is also no charge of tax if the source of income has ceased in the year before the payment is made.

Corporations are taxed on normal profits and are taxed on capital gains at a lower rate. The British tax authorities (the Inland Revenue) distinguish between corporations and individuals. Individuals pay tax applied on a progressive basis, in that the rate increases as the income increases. Corporations are charged at a set rate. The avoidance of taxes is not an allowable reason for setting up a business transaction in a particular manner. Thus, another business reason must be used for the structuring of the transaction. If the transaction did reduce taxes payable, the taxpayer must prove that the intent was not to produce a reduction in taxes. They must prove that the reduction of tax was not the main reason for the transaction. The taxpayer must also state the additional explanation and prove that they are the major reasons behind the structuring used.

Each country has its own stated guidelines on the use of avoidance vs. evasion. It is important to understand that such guidelines do exist and are different from country to country. The tax traveller must navigate through the jungle of differing interpretations in their journey towards reducing taxes. As a result, it is essential that proper guidance through professional expertise be sought. The main guideline of adherence is to insure that the letter as well as the spirit of law in each related country is considered. As one can see from the above analysis, by having knowledge of the basic tax laws for various countries, such a variance of interpretation can be used to a taxpayer's advantage.

Characteristics of Tax Havens

We have now dealt with the various tools required for use in tax haven analysis. This section provides a general analysis of those factors that must be evaluated for choosing a tax haven. These factors are the general guidelines or characteristics that must exist in a tax haven for the development of a proper vehicle, able to function to a high level of sophistication. These characteristics are of paramount importance for the purpose of evaluating a tax haven and developing uses for them.

Communication Lines in General

Communication represents the essence of doing business in today's international society. The high-speed transactions of the international business community dictate that every minute counts where profit is concerned. Business Executives at the international level operate on the belief that time is money, therefore when instructions are given, they must be executed efficiently and promptly, otherwise a company loses profits in terms of lost opportunities and lost cost savings. In the use of tax havens, it is essential that contact can be established with ease and without delay.

The standard communication lines on an international scale are postal service, telex service, telephone service, telegraph service and the Internet through Cyberspace, and businesses are use these mediums of communication as the norm. They must be present in every tax haven for proper communication. Without these services, the range of flexibility is reduced and efficient operation is dependent on fewer options, and increases the risk of doing business in that country. The higher the risk of doing business, the less favourable the use of that particular country.

Postal Service

The degree of efficiency of operation relates to the internal and external postal facilities. Post must travel within the country and internationally from country to country, and logically if such a service in a particular country is susceptible to frequent strikes, there could extended periods where the service is inoperative. The quality of the working postal system is also important: is mail sorted and delivered with promptness and efficiency? What are the chances of a letter or document arriving at its destination? When the document is sent to that country, or from that particular country, there must be a reliable postal service to insure that documents arrive on a timely basis and to the required destination. Some businesses have large volumes of business transactions and therefore require not only reliable but also high-speed postal service. In evaluating such a system, one must look at the degree of sophistication of the existing system and its quality of operation.

Telex/Facsimile Machine

Many businesses use a telex or fax machine for the efficient transmittal of business information and commands. Since businesses require frequent transmittal of legal documents, it is normally acceptable that a fax with a proper signature facility is acceptable as legal documents until the original arrives through another medium. Facsimiles eliminate most of the need for postal service, as information is transferred quickly and accurately. The question is how good is the system for facsimiles in the tax haven, as well as the quality of the phone service. Inadequate lines lead to poor quality transmissions, hence delays A client should also be concerned with the mechanisms in place for confidentiality, as many persons potentially have access to secured documents when they are faxed.

Telephone

Speaking on the telephone was the communication system of the 20th century. Most business is still conducted through this medium, although Cyberspace is slowly taking over. Currently, most Internet services require a telephone line to transmit its signals, though this is slowly moving towards more sophisticated means. Therefore, it is essential that such lines exist and are efficient so that there are no backlogs or delays that could prevent efficient business practice. Another potential problem is line interruption and line delays. Even if local telephone lines are operational, the question is whether international operations or communications are easily used, easily accessible, and can support high tech computer technology. Some countries have limited service, habitually in need of repair. Cell or mobile phones are extremely common, but there are always questions of confidentiality and security.

Telegraph

Another facility for the evaluation of communication lines is the telegraph system. The telegraph system is slowly being taken over by the use of the Internet and the use of facsimile machines. Such a system is usually a good substitute for a facsimile or telex, though there is a problem on secrecy and confidentiality regarding transmittal of information over such lines. Accessibility to such facilities is usually where the problem occurs. Some parts of the world still rely on this form of communication for doing business.

The Internet

Cyberspace is the system of the present and the future. Its expansion is increasing exponentially. In North America and Europe, almost every household has Internet access, in some form or another. If a business does not have an e-mail address or access to the Internet, they are viewed as technically inefficient, and their operation is viewed as unsophisticated in their equipment and not worthy of transacting business. The use of Cyberspace has just begun to take hold of the global business community. What has recently been dubbed *e-commerce* is already widespread, yet will continue to explode as the biggest business revolution in a century. As concern is raised over confidentiality and hacking, new secure measures are developed almost on a daily basis.

Transportation

At times in the course of a business year, it becomes a necessity to visit those countries where an entity is conducting business transactions, and the use of a tax haven presents another area where a firm or individual is actually transacting business. Physical presence accords assurance about the entire set-up in the location where business is being transacted. A tax haven country must have proper transportation links to allow for this business requirement. The categories used to rate the quality of transportation are the existence of daily flights, direct service, travel time, number of air carriers that service the country, availability of ground transportation, other modes of transportation, and dependability of all modes of transportation. Certain tax havens, such as Andorra, do not have an airport (in the case of Andorra it could be argued that this is not necessary, as there is an abundance of roads and trains connecting it to France). In most situations, the absence of an airport can create serious obstacles to large-scale business, for obvious reasons. It should be noted that the island tax havens mentioned in this book will be strictly rated in terms of air and boat service, as adequate ground transportation in most circumstances is non-existent, though boat service can also be quite slow.

For air transportation, the existence of daily flights to and from the haven provide easy accessibility, especially if a business crisis arises (and they do). Direct service for planes usually means that there is less chance of delays or missed connections. Some tax havens countries have an air service that is questionable in quality, with inconvenience as far as lateness of flights, misappropriation of luggage, and risks regarding the quality of aircraft used are the result.

Being able to travel in a swift fashion to the tax haven destination also increases accountability.

Travel time requires special consideration, regardless of mode. Our fast-moving society tends to dictate how easy business can be done. Quality of transportation is therefore a product of the modes of transportation available, as well as the number of carriers for each, and the greater the number, the more options are available. Finally, the dependability of all modes of transportation is an overriding factor in the quality. The country may possess many carriers and modes, yet if all these factors are not dependable, the greater the risks to one's business interests.

Political Stability

Political stability relates to a two-fold general criteria. When one refers to political stability, it is strongly connected to economic stability. Political stability in a host state can either fortify or decrease tax haven capabilities. If political and economic stability do not exist, other factors must be very strong for a tax traveller to contemplate the use of that tax haven. To illustrate the importance of this situation, one illustration would be the example of the relations between Ireland and Canada. The treaty between these two states provides respectable tax advantages. Ireland has been a country subjected to social and political turmoil in the past, though recently political change and an increased investment from the European Union have improved matters considerably. These factors can be nullified very quickly if there is a major political upheaval. Traditionally, the Irish situation has been very volatile, creating somewhat of a risk factor, but this has improved dramatically.

Some general criteria for evaluating political and economic stability are:

1. stability of currency
2. history of neutrality
3. lack of government intervention
4. conservative banking laws
5. a sound backing for its currency
6. international recognition as a business centre
7. freedom of currency movement
8. attitude of the people towards foreign intervention

The above list contains the most vital tests professionals recommend. It is important that the government and people of a tax haven and all other internal political factions be committed to the benefits of the tax haven and to the overall economy of that country. It is best that there have been very few insurrections in the past and not likely to be any in the future. Popular elections are vital, as this is usually an indication of stability as well as a democratic approach in a business economy. It is best that there be equitable distribution of wealth within the country, as a poorer state has a greater risk of popular resentment and corruption. Racial and religious harmony is also important, as the lack of such is an indication of potential problems.

Any instability or political problems increases the risk and greatly reduces the desirability of the country as a tax haven. A popular election is an indicator that government policies are supported by a majority of the population. The world has a history of unrest, and it appears that the majority of these wars or interactions were racially or religiously motivated. One can only say, that the past is a good indication of the future. With internal racial and religious harmony, the risk of political instability is greatly reduced.

Attitudes by Nationals towards Foreign Tax Travellers

Countries that welcome and thrive on tax haven activities are less likely to change their policies concerning investment enterprise from foreigners. For example, Monaco goes out of its way to accommodate tax travellers, many of whom are famous people. They make special allowances for celebrities such as actors and sports figures regarding residence and other benefits. There is little possibility that these personalities would encounter any risk in Monaco, as they are openly welcomed and accepted. This is true for any country, if a specific group of owners is welcomed and accepted by the nationals, and the risk of changing favourable laws against such factions is reduced.

It is always preferable to be in a jurisdiction that welcomes and thrives on the tax haven activities, as they are more inclined to keep special allowances that insure the clients are satisfied. This also reduces the likelihood that the situation would change, as any person using a country that has favourable tax laws, but are not as accommodating towards foreigners, could expect sudden changes in the tax laws that could prove harmful. In most tax havens, there are special laws strictly for foreign corporations who park their assets in that country. Although there are special laws for foreigners in these countries, in many of the countries the people and corporations that operate within the country are taxed normally.

Business Practices

Risk is not the only factor considered when making a choice of tax haven. A country offering special tax rates must also possess the basic commercial sophistication to handle the wealth tax travellers, and their complex operations, would bring with them. The basic commercial sophistication would include conditions and facilitates that would insure the safeguarding of assets. The usefulness of a tax haven is only as good as the sophistication of its commercial structure. Such sophistication involves the following components:

1. reliable banks
2. expert advice
3. freedom from unnecessary bureaucratic restraints
4. a proper legal structure
5. modern technological features

Tax havens are used by tax travellers who do not normally spend a great deal of their time in the tax haven to manage their own affairs. For these clients, the ideal haven would be one where the legal and commercial structure is modern, well tried and well seasoned. The formation of such operations should be a routine proposition, and necessary to such operation is these trustworthiness and credibility of the person or persons managing the clients' investments. Great care must be taken in the selection of these persons and tax travellers must always be aware of all avenues available to prosecute those who misuse funds and investments. This adds an element of protection to the tax traveller's assets.

The tax haven is only as good as the advisers and administrators managing the foreign holdings. The perfect example of this was the Turks and Caicos. These are small islands 600 miles south of Miami, in the Caribbean. The islands have very favourable tax laws, yet they did not have the quality of business practices required for performance of the necessary functions. Luckily, this has changed and the islands have come a long way and is a viable choice as an offshore location. When the Turks and Caicos first started out as a tax haven, the facilities and sophistication of professionals was questionable.

Switzerland, Liechtenstein and the Channel Islands have been tax havens for many years. They are examples of the most stable and sophisticated facilities for use by tax travellers. Switzerland being at the top of the pack among these is a result of its exceptional banking facilities.

Exchange Controls

Exchange control is also essential for tax haven consideration. Restrictions on convertability and transfer of funds could render any tax haven unworkable. If there are currency restrictions, profit can be rendered irrelevant. If the funds cannot be used they are meaningless. Many tax havens have exchange controls, but exemptions are provided for so-called tax travellers. This allows them to deal freely in any currency, move unlimited funds outside of the country, and conduct outside business without the fear or of any intervention.

Foreign currency management is an added bonus feature. An entity must have controlled its own foreign currency holdings to be able to effectively operate. The last thing a client would want is the requirement to hold funds in the local currency and have the funds potentially lose significant value. Tax havens usually meet this requirement by granting freedom from such control for all transactions outside their territory, or all transactions not linked with the territory. Formally, such regulations are usually independent of tax legislation. However, informally there are strong connections between the two in practice. Characteristically, one can expect strong exchange controls in high-tech jurisdictions and freedom from such controls in less economically established tax havens.

A good haven will be one that has no exchange controls for a tax traveller. This would allow the tax traveller to maintain several foreign currency bank accounts as well as relative freedom of desired foreign exchange management guidelines. A free flow of profits and payments will be afforded to the client. This freedom must be extended for a reasonable period of time to be effective, thus in evaluating a tax haven, the tax traveller will be looking for:

1. The existence of foreign exchange controls
2. The probability of controls being continued.

Secrecy

In most countries, one of the main terms for business, between banker and customer, is that all affairs and dealings are governed by the principal of secrecy. This principle is not new in today's society. Lawyers, accountants and doctors are governed by professional ethics dictating secrecy for client affairs. Recently, common law has shown that the principal of solicitor-client privilege is the strongest principle. Accountants and doctors relationships with clients have proven in courts to not be as solid or reliable. In many tax haven countries, the employees of the banks and other financial institutions are required to sign a declaration of secrecy regarding the business clients of the institution. It is suggested that this is not complete protection. Unfortunately, the only way to protect against such disclosure is to insure that a minimum number of people are aware of ownership.

Numbered accounts and use of nominee shareholders and directors are techniques used to maintain such standards. Most tax havens have such laws allowing for this, and they also sometimes use nominee shareholders and bearer shares. The state without secrecy laws, written or unwritten, will not be successful as a haven. This doctrine is an integral part of the ability of many havens to entice foreign investment. Set standards are relatively easy to maintain by ensuring the exchange of information is not in any of its treaties. Any haven without an existing tax treaty has an even greater appearance of relative security of such rights, although the absence of a tax treaty can hinder other potential savings. The Swiss banks were not the first to offer their clients substantial secrecy.

Generally, secrecy involves the amount and type of information available to the public. Laws that allow for the maintenance of the anonymity of the true owner of assets helps maintain these principles. A country cannot allow bank records to be open to tax authorities nor can they allow the requirement of filing of minutes or financial statements. Thus, in many tax havens there is no requirement for the filing of minutes or financial statements; financial information is merely for the outside party to pay a fee to maintain the active status of a corporation or Trust. The main interest in maintaining such secrecy is the ability to refrain from disclosure or leakage of any information.

One might generally question whether maintenance of security is possible in light of the current exertion of strength by major powers on such small countries that consider themselves tax havens. Most tax havens are very small states without much major clout in world politics. Can these small countries maintain set secrecy laws when confronted by a major power? For example, the Cayman Islands draw most of their business from the United States. If the US really needed information about a particular tax traveller, would this small country be susceptible to pressure by the US revenue authorities? The US could change or restrict all dealings with the Cayman Islands if they saw fit. Just recently, the Internal Revenue Service and their investigators managed a sting operation to find out information about the holdings of a US banker in a tax haven. Whether one thinks this is reasonable or not, other influences can be exerted on officials, as such information is never absolutely protected. Employees talk, and business associates and friends have a tendency to reveal information under social conditions. The Swiss, for example, have maintained secrecy of bank accounts for years, even to recent controversial revelation. If the tax authorities of another country can prove evasion under Swiss law, the Swiss are prepared to provide information about that person (it is worth noting that evasion under Swiss Law is closer to the standard definition of fraud, as the Swiss believe in the right to reduce taxes).

Influences of Major Powers

One of the least considered requirements of a tax haven is the potential influence of a major power on the operation of the haven in question. If a tax haven is under unofficial protection of a major power, can this power exert any influence on the country? If the tax haven receives a large amount of funding from a major power or is in some other ways connected economically, the major power may be in a position to influence policy decisions of the haven. Under these conditions, when the major power finds it is losing a large amount of tax dollars to this country, they can do something to change the situation. For example, in the 1980s the US tax authorities initiated a special study group studying the use of tax havens. If this group found that excessive American dollars were going to the Cayman Islands (or any other tax haven) or the Bahamas, one can be assured that stringent measures would have been be implemented.

What the IRS would actually do is not known, but the political power of the US can be exerted on these tiny countries to implement policy changes. The US not only provides tax travellers for these countries, but it also provides most of their tourist income and construction loans. As a result of economic and political influence the Unite States.

has a special type of indirect control over many countries. All goods used by many of these countries are actually shipped from the US. The changing of any of the supply lines could hurt them.

Another alternative that has already been used by the Americans was to change their tax policy regarding inventories held outside the US, and this was exerted on certain Caribbean islands. If the US tax authorities were to decide that any dealings with tax havens should be deemed a sham (a sham being any transaction in their opinion that is merely smoke and mirrors to hide the true reason for a transaction: the reduction or avoidance of taxation), there would be a dramatic shift of sheltered dollars from these countries. Britain and the Channel Islands are another similar example. The UK also has major influence on many other tax havens, such as the British Virgin Islands, Bermuda and the Turks and Caicos. The question that cannot be answered is whether or not the major powers would actually implement such destructive influence. It seems likely that such powerful states have too much concern for the global economy to implement such destructive forces.

The recommended criteria for evaluating the influence of a major power contains the following:

1. Does the haven have a special relationship with a foreign power that could ultimately interfere in its tax haven status (i.e. dependency on foreign powers)?
2. Is the internal legislative body conscious of maintenance of separate national identity (independent legislative system)?
3. Detail any influence of foreign business interests. If the user currency is that of a major power (i.e. a Caribbean island using US dollars), there is an amount of influence that can be exerted (that is influence from an independent financial sector).

Political Relations with Other Countries

Political relations exercised by a tax haven can be very important to its existence in the international market. Logically, the major economic powers will be more sympathetic to the needs and problems of a state that they have favourable relations with. Tax havens are characteristically very small countries and size makes it imperative that they have good relations with all major powers as well as their neighbouring countries. For such a relationship to exist there must be an inherent compatibility of political structure and ideology. That is not to say there must be a similar general philosophy. For example, in the past the United States and the United Kingdom were reluctant to invest behind the Iron Curtain. Currently, the new Russian Federation has opened its doors to a democratic system that has resulted in a major influx of Western-style business, internally and externally. Investing in such a country, it is believed, would be helping such a state, in the fledgling stages of growth, to prosper.

Recently, China has opened its doors, yet they have been slow to change their underlying political philosophy, while at the same time making the minute gestures towards becoming a free market economy. This has created guarded investment by democratic countries, led by the United States. There remains fear regarding the protection of investment assets, but as China continues to prove itself as a viable market, that investment will continue to explode. Likewise, if the internal politics of the haven are considered as socially repressive, businesspeople would tend to be reluctant to invest as a natural reaction regarding the protection of their own assets. As political incompatibility between the tax haven state and the major power lessens, the investment level and trust in that haven increases.

If the tax haven country is involving itself in the politics of neighbouring states, the influence of any major power might bring it into the middle of a volatile situation. This could affect its own ability to operate as a separate autonomous tax haven. In recent years, Britain tends to stay away from the internal policies of its former colonies, such as the British Virgin Islands, Bermuda, and Canada, only intervening upon occasion over matters of security. Perhaps this explains why a majority of the current tax havens are former British colonies or protectorates.

Treaties

The final characteristic to be evaluated is that of the tax treaty. The existence (or non-existence) of tax treaties is important when choosing a tax haven. Some tax havens owe their existence to the fact that they are a party to tax treaties. The Netherlands Antilles is a prime example of this. These countries possess unique qualities that allow the existence of treaties, namely they have enough strength internally to maintain their position under pressure from other countries. The Netherlands Antilles is under the strong protection of the Netherlands, who have a large amount of tax treaties with other nations of the world. The philosophy of the Netherlands serves to enhance the existence of the Netherlands Antilles and their tax haven status. The Netherlands also protects the status of this haven in its dealings with other nations. This unique situation allows the existence of treaties to be a benefit. Switzerland is another country that enjoys this benefit. The country is so strong economically that its existence cannot be challenged. As a result, Switzerland is able to maintain their status as a tax haven, as well as effectively negotiate numerous tax treaties with other nations of the world.

In general, most businesspeople find that the non-existence of tax treaties is to their benefit. This status has an impact on the ability of the tax traveller to maintain anonymity, as tax treaties usually either require or imply an exchange of information between the participants. Most clients require this vital secrecy. However, there are exceptions to this philosophy, as with the example of Grenada, enjoying a tax treaty with the United States for disclosure of information that is in the possession of the government. The key to this treaty is the requirement that the government need only disclose what information is in their possession. If the government does not possess information about individuals, corporations or Trusts within their country, they cannot disclose them. Thus, they do not require the filing of such information that can identify the parties involved or the financial structure.

Considerations regarding the evaluation of the benefit or non-benefit of having tax treaties are as follows:

1. If the country the haven has a treaty with is a major power, the treaty could have an extremely negative impact on usefulness of the tax haven.
2. If the country the haven has a treaty with is another tax haven, secrecy will usually be guaranteed.
3. If the country is not a major power, the impact is of a lesser degree.
4. The treaty might only relate to certain business arrangements (i.e. Luxembourg has eight treaties, none of which include the treatment of holding companies).

Other Characteristics to Be Evaluated

Seven other characteristics that can be important in evaluating the usefulness of a tax haven are:

1. The variety of uses of that tax haven

2. Distances to the tax haven.

3. Standard of living in the tax haven.

4. Banking facilities within that country, and connections with banking facilities in other countries.

5. Residency rules of the tax haven and any home country involved.

6. The attitude of tax authorities in other countries, especially the home country.

7. Reliability of business functions within the tax haven.

Having a variety of uses available to the tax traveller is an obvious advantage. The more uses available, the greater the number of situations that can be handled through the tax haven. The tax traveller would obviously like a haven that allows maximum flexibility. Certain havens restrict the uses by catering to a specific type of individual or other criteria. Monaco and Costa Rica favour individuals, Luxembourg looks to holding companies, and Liberia favours shipping companies. The client must be sure of their wishes if they are to rely on a tax haven with restricted use. In the case of restricted use, the client's personal preference becomes very important in the decision-making process. The distance from the tax traveller's main operations to the tax haven is also a factor. The client located in Britain will not go to the South Pacific if there is a choice of two havens with equal benefit, and one haven is closer. When the final choice is difficult to make, distance might become a major characteristic for the final decision.

Standard of living in the tax haven and banking facilities are important considerations for the tax traveller intending to visit the tax haven. If the client intends to periodically visit the haven that they are using, they would want available facilities to be of sufficient quality to make the visit pleasant, as well as profitable. A good standard of living is also a factor in determining the level of competence for conducting business. A country with a low standard of living lacks the business and professional expertise required in international circles. Proper banking facilities are always a must for tax haven activities. It is also important that the major banks are internationally recognised. This would allow for ease of movement of funds as well as providing the tax traveller with confidence in the quality of the system.

Most tax travellers are not interested in residence in the tax haven. This is only a consideration for the rare client who, in addition to finding a haven, is looking also for a base to set up their operation, and either desire the haven location or want to live near their business. The attitude of tax authorities in other countries is also important when a tax traveller is deciding whether they want to avoid all contact with such people. If the tax authorities in the country where the tax traveller has their operation, feel that any dealings with the particular tax haven is a sham transaction (see previous definition), the traveller knows they will be given trouble if they channel their operations there. Such authorities will question every move or contact made with the tax haven, and could create untold grief for the tax traveller. The Government of Australia, for example, has a blacklist of tax havens. This list of infamous havens sports those states the Australian tax authorities look at with suspicion. If one operates through Australia, it is wise to avoid the blacklisted havens, as dealing with them could result in trouble with the Australian tax authorities. Finally, It is important that staff are reliable and businesses conducted smoothly and efficiently, and without interruption at the tax haven location. All of these contribute to insure that, not only the laws of the tax haven are effective, but that they can be implemented with some degree of efficiency and effectiveness.

Specific Characteristics

Up to this point, a general analysis of all characteristics that must be evaluated has been given. As one can determine, there are many other variables and important criteria that can be used in evaluating the suitability of a base operation in a tax haven. A standard analysis would have a difficult time taking into account every single characteristic required. It is the intent of this book to provide a decision-making rationale for the reader to us in evaluating what is important. Although reference is made to specific countries throughout, these are only for illustrative purposes only, and are not a reflection of any endorsement of one country or another. Farther on in this book, a specific, brief analysis of several home countries (or base countries, as they may be called) will be given. This discussion will also be of a general nature, as the details of the law of any particular country would involve a core text of its own. In conjunction with these general characteristics, it is useful to look at some of the more specific considerations as well.

International Commerce

Credit is a very important consideration when doing business domestically and internationally. Foreign exchange and various currencies add further complications to the credit problem. Credit is considered one of the major driving engines for international commerce and exists in conjunction with major multinational and financial institutions. Thus it is important for a country to have a solid credit reputation in order for business to be done with ease. If a country's credit rating drops, it loses some of its attractiveness and certain companies might want to move their location. Some say that it is absolutely important that a strong credit rating exists and is essential for a tax haven. This is not always the case, but it is a good general rule.

Another consideration relates to the ability of businesspeople to move and meet in locations all around the world. Many of the tax havens are pursuing their desire to become successful, first rate business centres by promoting their country abroad. In many respects they are coming into their own and becoming recognised locations for business to operate. For example, the country of Grenada has just started to follow states such as Panama, Colon, Ireland, the New Hebrides and the Cayman Islands in promoting their country as a favourable location for business. Their initial efforts will be directed to North America and certain parts of Europe. Grenada, in the past few years, has attracted over 1,500 companies to their shores. Such efforts have been a result of private initiatives; it would seem most beneficial for them if their governments set up offices in major economic states, with the sole intention of promoting their country for business (i.e. most tax havens have tourism consulates).

Such agencies facilitate promotional activities internationally, through brochures, seminars and special trade visits by delegations, publicising the benefits of their state. The main conditions they emphasise are the strong economic, political, legal and business backgrounds of the particular country concerned. Those wanting to use such tax haven countries should be familiarising themselves with the unique laws of that country, helping to determine if favourable conditions exist. Based on these laws, it is beneficial to analyse the vehicles available and be able to marry these vehicles with those of other tax havens to put together a solid international structure that is to the benefit of the user.

Fair Treatment

There are many developing nations that have historically been discouraging to foreign interests, making it difficult to take advantage of their benefits. Such an unwelcome atmosphere is not as easy to recognise as may be imagines, as those in official positions may welcome business and see the potential benefits to that country, yet the local people resent the attitude and wealth of these foreigners. As an example, it has been observed in years past that certain Caribbean countries had an underlying feeling of distrust towards the haven-seekers, and widespread overcharging of local services was rampant. Exorbitant fees for a simple task, such as a standard land title registration, was a common occurrence.

Although times have changed for the better, a deeply entrenched attitude against foreigners can create a sinister and unpredictable atmosphere that is not beneficial to foreign intervention. Most tax haven states recognise the potential and obvious benefits in obtaining sufficient capital for development, and increasing the wealth internally through the influx of foreign currency and foreign spending. Unfortunately, a thorough investigation of the tax haven location must occur, as it has been demonstrated that the officials of the haven could be far more welcoming and accepting of foreign elements than the general population. As an example, it is widely known that in many parts of the globe, justified or not, there is resentment towards the prosperity of Americans. US apologists claim it is a jealousy for a better life or better economic position that fuels the tension. Problems have developed in such countries as Jamaica, where the poverty of many is mirrored by the prosperity of few.

It has been suggested that to measure the degree of acceptance of investment from overseas, one should scrutinise the foreign investment laws, though this is not always the case. Luckily, for most

Caribbean countries, time has healed wounds, and foreign investment laws that are favourable for outside business personnel are a result of a popular acceptance of foreigners into their country. In fact, in many countries, foreign capital is treated the same as domestic investment.

Fair treatment is a subjective mystery. Some governments consider fair treatment as limiting the freedom of activity within the tax haven. For example, Switzerland limits their special status to foreign companies that do not have a majority of their activities or derive a majority of their revenue domestically. Another example is Mexico, which limits foreign enterprises and industry to a certain level of investment. Canada for example, gives special tax breaks to Canadian corporations that are owned by a majority of Canadians. This in fact does not give fair treatment to foreign-owned corporations operating in Canada. It is reasonable to say that ownership restrictions and other fairness restrictions are best when they allow a greater effective level of flexibility for an enterprise to operate independently, and to conduct normally accepted business practices.

Investment Concessions

Another area of investment in developing countries has been through the encouragement of foreign set-up of businesses, with various kinds of commercial or industrial concessions. Investment concessions are usually given on a case-by-case basis and are not necessarily a true indication of an offshore centre. Due to the localised and particular nature of the situation, the special tax benefits only relate to a particular company, their operation and details, as determined by a distinct contract. Many tax havens do not restrict themselves to particular contracts, but try to make concessions regarding investments through financing and trading where the goods are not produced within their country. Multinationals will usually seek out these incentives when they are trying to establish where they should create and sustain an overseas operation.

Guarantees

A host government must give a holding company fair treatment, as it is a prime attraction for the international investors. Fair treatment might not be that important if that country is politically unstable. If there is a potential problem internally, either from the threat of uprising, military coup, or invasion by another country, even regardless of the stability of the state, any guarantee given cannot be relied upon with as much assurance as one would like. There is always the potential for a new incumbent government not wanting foreign investment and seizing all assets within its borders, so politics within and the potential for drastic political change are important on guarantees made. There are many examples of this happening throughout history, some within Central America (i.e. Honduras, Nicaragua, etc.), South America, the Caribbean and in Eastern Europe.

Another danger regarding instability is the prospect of new legislation or government regulatory action being enacted to change things for the future. As already explained, most tax havens are small countries, and if they are not highly dependent on trade with major nations of the world, they can easily change or manipulate their laws within a short period of time. This creates major problems for foreign businesses located in the haven. It is one of the most dangerous prospects that loom over all tax havens. In situations where a new government comes to power, bringing new legislation, and those in power have offered a settlement, the client may have far less choices at hand. Thus, it might be important to have guarantees against expropriation or nationalisation. Many experts on offshore centres advocate this, but it is this author's opinion that such guarantees may be of little importance when political changes or turmoil occur. One cannot go to the new government, if there has been an insurrection, and hope for success with a claim that the former government has made guarantees, without major influence and power over the new regime. International law has cases where revolutionary governments refused to honour agreements made by the previous political leadership.

Many of countries are realising the need for such safeguards to attract foreign capital and investment. They have offered a guarantee as part of their incentive against other problems. These built-in protections against expropriation in guarantee transfer capital and profits can be very important. In any event, no matter what the guarantee, the foreign company must always be on guard. They must ensure that an adviser is monitoring the situation at all times and a mechanism exists for the movement of assets on a quick and easy basis where political instability is a possibility. It is claimed that an individual can apply to the government, through finance or commerce, for a guarantee to be given on a case-by-case basis. Many tax haven countries will be happy to furnish such a written guarantee that the assets of the investor will not be nationalised for any reason. If there is instability this may be of no consequence. Such guarantees are only of consequence where the country is stable, and the guarantee is merely a mechanism to insure that laws are changed and assets are appropriated. Thus, for a country that has been around for many years and has developed a reputation for integrity, such guarantees are of significance. They provide a backup for recovery of any losses if any changes are implemented. As we move further and further towards a global economy, an element of stability will be derived through the influence of monitoring of business practices by international organisations. The United Nations and other governing bodies, including the World Trade Organisation, will hopefully gain enough strength as we move to an international business community to ensure that any guarantees are upheld globally.

International business is becoming more and more important as we are moving towards a global economy. With this, the strength or instability of so-called tax havens is increased and the guarantee against loss of assets to foreign investors is also strengthened. It is expected that the advent of bilateral agreements, risk guarantees, and other international agreements will serve to provide stability to business on an international level, once a stronger global economy is established.

Low Taxes

Many people look at tax havens and think that the biggest attraction of these countries is their low taxes, but this is not quite as lucrative as it once was. Certainly, lower taxes are still a major consideration. Some of the tax havens have in recent years raised their tax on corporations to raise more money, though the amount is negligible in comparison to what the companies would be paying in their home country. Without going into specific details on the tax laws of particular countries, an in-depth analysis of countries such as Panama, Cuba, the United States and others will demonstrate that low taxes is still an important consideration. Many countries that were previously considered tax havens are no longer such, as a result of changes in their tax rate. These countries have increased their taxation, specifically so that low tax is not the main incentive. They recognise that other investment incentives, such as a stable government, availability of labour, communication lines, access by travel, and other factors have led to the offshore's attractiveness, without the need to cut their own revenues by having low taxes.

Double Taxation Treaties

A taxpayer would always want to avoid any instance of double taxation. This is true domestically as well as internationally. On an international scale, the avoidance of double taxation is the main reason that a country negotiates a tax treaty. Therefore, in appearance, it seems that the more tax treaties a country has the better it is. In many cases this is true, but there are times when this is not. Another benefit of tax treaties is that they encourage trade among the countries involved. Unfortunately, many tax havens do not have the economic strengths to be in the position to properly negotiate a fair tax treaty. One method of overcoming this is through the use of an intermediary country. For example, the Netherlands is a very strong country economically and has negotiated a broad system of favourable tax treaties. The Netherlands Antilles, discussed previously, was a possession of the Netherlands, and were able to take advantage of a strong treaty system with their home country and develop a low tax and tax haven status. As a result, the Netherlands and Netherlands Antilles are frequently used by many international companies for the avoidance or reduction of taxes. Switzerland and Belgium are other countries that have highly developed networks of treaties. For those former British colonial tax havens, the United Kingdom has an extensive network of tax treaties.

The United States Treasury has been negotiating changes regarding their conventions with various industrial nations. Of significance, the Treasury is very much concerned with countries where bank secrecy principles are practised, and they have been making efforts to circumvent secrecy laws, such as the Swiss Bank secrecy laws that restrict access to information about corporations or individuals. The US does not believe that other states should be allowed to restrict such information, and is thus attempting to change the treaty clauses providing for the reservation on secrecy of information and state rights. Highly critical of treaty provisions refusing exchange of information to protect its businesses and individuals as a result of security or public policy, the US intends on amendment of such as foreign policy. The American position is that income tax conventions with Switzerland and other countries are very important, therefore it is equally important to negotiate an agreement on the scope of an application of the exchange of information. If one looks at their attempts to renegotiate, it is clear that the US is actually attempting to change the previous conditions and allow for full access to information that would curtail the secrecy policies. The US does not stand alone in these attempts and they are more than willing to use their power to force the other parties to their treaties into a conciliatory measure.

What they are really seeking is to break the backs of old, so-called tax havens by removing the confidentiality and anonymity provisions that tax havens preciously protect. In reality, Canada the US and other countries are moving towards implementing these laws, whether or not disclosure of foreign holdings would produce a profit or loss. The US has started a move towards what is called the *treaty-based return position*, requiring a special return that shows the calculation of taxes owing if a treaty wasn't in existence. This difference they call a treaty-based return position. One can look also at the Canadian authorities and others, who are sure to move towards such a position as well. The US is also requiring special reporting requirements for foreign taxpayers that do business in United States. This type of return requires them to disclose all the facts of their business and transactions. It is obvious that upon the reporting of such facts or foreign investment information, a taxpayer or corporation would merely be invoking an investigation by the Revenue authorities.

Similar provisions exist in Canada as well. The danger of taking such a position is that they will encourage more people to be disgruntled with the system and avoid any type of disclosure that could create a potential problem. Revenue authorities appear oblivious to the fact that as they choke the public with more rules and regulations, ultimately resulting in more taxes and great bureaucratic aggravation, they are merely creating a larger base of individuals and corporations that not report their red flag activities. Individuals and corporations are reaching their saturation point at which they are willing to tolerate such requirements. Such efforts on the part of revenue officials in various countries will also only serve to create a larger base of tax travellers who will not only move their operations elsewhere, but employ people in other countries. This would serve to reduce the personal tax revenue base that provides the bulk of government revenue. An additional effect would be less spending by corporations and their senior executives and employees within that jurisdiction. In the end, a country's economy would suffer.

The US tax treaties have been exercised to negotiate an exchange of information, in an attempt to stop this loss of revenue. However, they need to watch that they are not curtailing the incentive to do business abroad, as such actions will directly affect the strength of their economy. The required exchange of information is normally restricted to what is in the possession of the governments involved. In many offshore centres, there is no real requirement to file financial information or the names of shareholders of a company. The use of bearer shares and nominee shareholders, and no financial filing, would render treaty disclosures useless, as the government does not possess information that is relevant. They would have to include disclosure of private information as well.

The US and a few other powers have embarked on a crusade against such tax havens. Such moves are generally opposed internationally, as they could create major problems for the small economies in these countries. A major effort was conducted to have a Multilateral Mutual Assistance Agreement between the major nations and the tax havens that have implied connections to them. This agreement was intended to target determination of income sources, allocation of expenses, and disclosure of relevant information to trace the parties involved and their locations. Many have referred to this move as an attempt to impose an international police force on these sovereign countries. The treaty would put pressure on the main country (i.e. the UK) to compel those whom it has ties with to provide the required information. Fortunately, Canada, France, Germany, Netherlands, Switzerland and the UK have opposed this measure. The main proponent of this is the United States, and since most of the popular tax haven destinations are tied to the UK and the Netherlands, perhaps this measure will not have such a widespread negative effect.

Yet another vehicle considered for diminishing the lucrative lure of offshore entities is one proposed by the Europeans. They want to impose what is called a *common withholding tax*. This is a dangerous notion that could have very negative consequences on the states of the European Union. The imposition of a withholding tax by one country has a history of benefiting the other countries not imposing the tax. In the past, the US had imposed such a tax on some of its funds and transactions that moved financing and goods abroad. This move served to enhance a faltering British financial structure at the expense of the US. Businesspeople simply went to Britain for financing. The proposal would impose the tax on all European Union members, including the UK, with the intention that they would then impose or pass the requirements to those countries that it has ties with. Most of the Caribbean or Cari-com countries have ties with the UK (i.e. the Cayman Islands, British Virgin Islands, Bermuda and the Turks & Caicos). There is a great deal of opposition to such a proposal as financiers are worried about its impact on the Euro. Others remember the past and feel such a move would greatly enhance the US and bolster an already strong US Dollar, as well as the US economy as a whole. As one could imagine, the UK is not one of the countries in favour of such a measure.

The US and the European Union (including member states individually) have implemented studies on methods to monitor activities of such offshore entities. Measures have been recommended to open up disclosure of ownership, as well as cracking down on offshore advisers and imposing disclosure on offshore Trust companies. It is therefore important to be aware of what influences there are on an offshore country and what sacrifices will be made locally. For example, is the offshore country so tied to the home country that it cannot afford to give up these ties in order to retain its special status? It is this author's opinion that such laws will only weed out the weaker states that are dependent on such ties, and strengthen those states less dependent on financial support. The small states listed previously that possess close ties to the UK would have to make such a decision. Others such as Grenada could resist and assert their independence.

Many offshore countries are highly sensitive upon outside encroachment on their freedom and could very well opt to sacrifice financial aid and ties to the home country in exchange for financial independence and freedom. It is also a general political and moral query whether major powers in a free global market should have the ability to exert such pressure and control over smaller states. A possible result of such measures will be the advent of the stronger international corporations backing such offshore countries financially in replacement of the regulatory ties of the main G7 governments.

The UK issued its white paper on its plan for the dependent territories in 1999. This can be found on the Internet at www.fco.gov.uk/news/newspage.asp?17/03/99.

On the other hand, there should be increased activities to curtail criminal activity such as money laundering, fraud, tax evasion and other abuses of the system. It is not fundamentally the intention of offshore countries to promote such activities, though they do occur nonetheless, sometimes aided by individuals in those countries. The question to be asked is what would be the cost of implementing such extreme measures. Such strong efforts (as suggested by the UK) are:

1. Regulation of offshore countries
2. Comprehensive measures to curtail money laundering by regulating company formation offshore and those involved in doing so
3. Co-operation with investigations
4. Establishing independent regulatory bodies to oversee these countries

These would only serve to strengthen the control of outside countries over the freedom of the independent offshore communities. Although the UK and US feel justified in trying to truncate offshore operations, these measures go to the very base of upsetting the notion of a free and democratic global society, with uncertain consequences. In criminal law, the laws are implemented in such a way that, although a percentage of criminals do not get caught, it ensures that the innocent are not falsely accused or incarcerated. It is our hope that in the effort to stop the few, we are not destroying the economies and the lives of the people of many of these offshore countries. It would appear that the intention of some powerful states is to inhibit such countries in their ability to create a stronger, self-sufficient economy. This perpetuate a world segregated between a few wealthy nations one side of the divide, and many poorer nations, totally dependent on the few wealthy ones for survival, on the other. This would be a regressive step backwards to the misguided economies of the past.

Restrictions by Government Regulations

For evaluating offshore centres, the degree of internal restrictions by regulatory bodies is important. The absence of regulations is usually a good indication of a strong and prosperous economy that the offshore traveller can rely upon for the safety of their assets. Government controls are the degree to which the government imposes, for example, exchange controls or any currency controls that might be imposed. As is obvious, the offshore client would like to see as little exchange or currency controls as possible. If a government does not have to exercise such controls, it is a good indication that the government and the international business community feel that the currency and economy are strong enough that such controls are not required to protect the domestic economy of that country. With some countries that impose exchange and currency controls, there is the possibility that a special deal can be negotiated for the alleviation or elimination of such controls. This measure would be on a case by case basis and would also be dependent on such conditions as the magnitude of influx of finances and assets, the overall desirability to attract such businesspeople to that country, and any other influence of relevance. The globalisation of the world market, which seems to be growing, will probably eliminate or reduce such controls as the world is moving to one or two standard currencies, such as the Euro or the US Dollar.

Another restriction that has been imposed is the import of materials or goods. This is usually designed to protect a domestic market where the locals might be at a disadvantage to any foreign operation that can obtain raw materials at a cheaper rate than the cost domestically. If the good was produced or available locally, such a move would severely hurt the domestic market, thus controls would be imposed. This problem usually occurs when the foreign operation is looking to set up operations domestically. If such is the case, it is not only important that there are no existing restrictions, they should consider the possibility of future restrictions imposed in the event that they are creating unwanted competition with a domestic producer. Other considerations for operating domestically are the change in low tax status that many countries make available only to foreigners that do not produce or market their products locally. The availability of all the necessary materials, transportation, labour and other conditions required to do business must also be considered. In evaluating the propensity of the government to impose restrictions, one should look at the dependence of the offshore country on trading as a source of gross domestic product. This is also true if trading is a main source used by the country to attract foreign companies. If such were the case, they would hurt their own economy by imposing restrictions and thus a lower likelihood of restrictions being imposed.

In general, an overall lack of government control serves to make a tax haven attractive to foreign operations. One method of doing this while preserving a local market is to impose a free-trade zone where such operations can set up and not have to worry about the imposition of regulations.

Bank Secrecy

Although discussed briefly at an earlier stage, it is important that this topic be dealt with in detail. The maintenance of bank secrecy is essential to the maintenance of confidentiality and anonymity that are the mainstays of an offshore location. There is a great deal of difference between the avenues of a country's secrecy laws for banks. Some countries impose bank secrecy through a legislative route and have specific laws passed within the local government and decreed as law in a written form. This usually takes the form of a Banking Act or similar legislation that includes banking as part of its contents.

The other method of imposing secrecy is through the common law (if a common law system is used). Common law is established by precedent, derived through the legal system of case law or through the normal accepted practice that is in place between institutions. Accepted practice can be considered as a form of contract, or in some cases, it is an actual contract. Under this approach, the parties to the contract can sue each other for breach of contract if the contract is breached. The validity of such contracts is becoming increasingly contentious and governments of home countries are stepping up challenges to the right to have such a contract. Most offshore countries impose heavy fines and jail terms for violation of such secrecy laws, although if it is legislatively backed its strength is increased.

There is a wise, old saying that "people talk". This is a truth, and no matter what level of law is used, it cannot overcome this reality. It is interesting that it is not normally the people in the institutions who do the talking - many times it is the actual user, their spouse, or business associates, and the most frequent venue for this is at social gatherings. Unhappy employees, jealousy and people's desire for recognition are the main causes of such problems. The IRS recently conducted a sting operation to find out about the holdings of a prominent banker in the US. In order to conduct the sting, they had to know who the person was (i.e. the Banker), what country they were located in and what the nature of the entity was. This information was initiated by leads from people around the individual at social gatherings and then ultimately by agents being planted socially at the offshore location. It all hinged on the initial contact, so when one worries about disclosure at the offshore location, they should be just as concerned with their own actions at home. Other sources of information are spouses, children and other relatives.

The US government has at times put pressure on major banks with branches in the offshore locations. It is thus important to pay for and get proper advice on the topic, and many times that information is free and readily available. The US has at times suggested that they should cut off airline service to countries that will not negotiate a treaty. It is worthwhile to note that many offshore countries do have agreements for exchange of information where drug abuse, fraud and criminal activities are present. It is important to note that each country might have a different definition of what fraud, drug abuse or criminal activity consists of. This exchange is restricted in the type of information that will be exchanged. For example, only tax information on earnings might be disclosed and not ownership. One must go to the treaty to determine this. An example of varying definitions is Switzerland, which does not have the same definition of tax evasion or fraud that the US might have. It is thus important to note in a treaty whether fraud is considered as being based on Swiss law or US law for determining the exchange of information. Many international agreements state the governing law that is to be applied.

Another trail that can be followed is when information about holdings is sent through the mail to the home country. Information about a company's Swiss Bank account can be flagged when there is frequent mail from Switzerland to a particular taxpayer or corporation. To maintain confidentiality, other means must be devised. It is important to note that any transaction with an *offshore tax haven* will be scrutinised by authorities, if they are aware of its existence. Although such offshore use is perfectly legal, if operations are examined by revenue authorities they are noted for creating major havoc with the user resulting in legal proceedings and harassment for many years and costing large amounts of dollars for something that could be perfectly legal. Revenue authorities in the US, Canada and other countries have not reached the point where they have to pay for any inconvenience caused, nor can the damage in most cases be measured. This is a strong reason why confidentiality and anonymity should be maintained. Loss of reputation is something that cannot be measured, whereas it has broken the back of many a strong person (see the numerous cases where the press and other media have falsely accused people and ruined their lives).

Another consideration for the promotion of offshore entities is the fact that in many cases the existing revenue laws are not strong enough to protect the individual or corporation. Such protection is required from abuse or loss or lack of documentary evidence in many cases where a person is innocent, yet the evidence does not exist anymore or it was never physically documented. This allows the authorities involved to fall back on statutory requirements for proper physical documentation. Revenue authorities should err on the side of the taxpayer not the reverse. This situation only makes the abuse of the system greater as people are tired of the constant unfairness. It should always be understood that the vast majority of businesses and persons want to pay their fair share of tax for the privilege of living in peace and comfort, as is their right. Most abuse of taxes owing is done domestically. The IRS has done studies to show a large part of the abuse is by local people and corporations who simply do not disclose or pay tax when owed.

Another problem with exchange controls is the inability of a company to pay dividends or to transfer exchange earnings. This is a major deterrent from the use of an offshore country. What is the use of savings if a company cannot distribute its profits to its owners, being the shareholders? Limitations on other items such as royalty returns and other payments are also deterrents. As was mentioned before, many of these controls can be circumvented through individual negotiation with the offshore government. This of course is not the most desirable alternative, but it is a valuable one. As the larger home countries negotiate or exert influence to require disclosure by some offshore states, these negotiated alternatives with less desirable havens, with no ties or pressure from a major power, will become a viable alternative.

Government co-operation is also a necessity in choosing an offshore country. There is a great deal of documentation that needs to be completed and the tax traveller is relying on the co-operation of the government to speed up the process and prevent regular business from slowing down to a stand still. With today's ever-increasing frequency and speed of transactions, using higher technology, the offshore country must be in line with business, and if not, they're a risky alternative. Hypothetically, the laws of an offshore could make it look favourable, yet if the government is not committed to promoting business and assisting them, the offshore would not be viable. This is true in any country, not just the offshore countries. The government must truly believe in the benefit of foreigners, their capital and benefit of their operations, and it is more important for a small country that the government shows a positive commitment, and not be passive in their actions.

There are many examples of countries that have not recognised this pro-active need or have simply wanted to change its status. Venezuela is an example of a government that has been rather lax in keeping a positive commitment, while some others merely were absorbed by a major power and, by attrition, relinquishing their status. There are many others that have gone the opposite way and promoted their country. Some countries wanted to restrict foreigners from populating their country so they restricted entrance or made it difficult to set foot on their soil, yet they have maintained a strong base for use as an offshore location. Nauru, for example, has managed to restrict access to their island by allowing most of the paper work required to flow through another location in Australia. Others have special territorial status for specific functions. Liberia restricted itself to shipping, yet it is unwise to visit their country. This is more a fact of caution than any restrictions imposed by the local government.

As can be seen from this brief analysis, there are many states considered offshore tax havens, with low tax laws that target a specific sector, such as artists and writers, celebrities, Trusts, or for foreign holding companies. Singapore has what is called a *territorial taxation system* that taxes mainly on profits within the territory.

It is important when evaluating or choosing a tax haven not to forget about some centres that favour a particular use or target a particular market. We tend to look at those that are broader based, yet there may be some that are more favourable for our special needs. Some of these special needs locations are Ireland, Singapore, Hong Kong, the Netherlands, Denmark, Thailand, France and even the Vatican. Those in the European Union may in future be affected by legislation. Also in Europe, Switzerland and Liechtenstein are the longest surviving tax havens and considered the strongest. Others locations are either moving towards more inviting laws or have small special uses, including Iceland, Campione, Trieste in Italy, Austria, Hungary, Chechnya in Russia, and Cyprus. In the Caribbean, such countries are Antigua, Bahamas, Barbados, Belize, British Virgin Islands, St. Vincent and of course Grenada (these countries all have special status for what is called an International Business Corporation (IBC)). Grenada is one of the fast risers and foreign investment is just starting to accelerate. Jamaica has not entered the realm of the others, as it has emphasised direct investment rather than holding or financing companies. The use of tax havens, with an analysis of the benefits of the more popular offshores, is the next aspect for evaluation.

Zones and Offshores

Free Trade Zones and Special Internal Services

Many people are not aware that some of the major powers (the US, for example) offer a number of zones within their state territories that cater to the needs of foreign investment. The US known for having more than a dozen of these zones, with specialised services. Perhaps the most notable are Delaware and Montana.

What are the benefits of these zones? The most obvious and strongest is that they are located in a country that is very stable politically and has a strong economy. They are relatively safe for transfer and investment of funds when compared to some of the other offshore jurisdictions. They also cater only to foreign individuals or corporations and thus can offer a strong, safe location to bank their assets. These zones advertise that they are available to all foreign vehicles, including corporations, Trusts, individuals, associations, partnerships and others. They feel that they can compete with offshore centres, as the risk of political instability, economic insecurity, and other financial problems are absent. I do not believe that these features are as important as they were at one time. We are moving towards a global economy and many of the offshore centres no longer pose such risks to investors. One strength American zones do provide is more protection for physical assets and, because they are not offshore, it is certainly easier for access, but they are available only to foreigners.

Montana, for example, is a major gold producer and a large source of platinum and palladium. Montana can therefore easily convert a customer asset from cash to a purchase of precious metals that can be used as a hedge against inflation. These special accounts are exempt from US taxation. The exemption extends to others, such as gems, works of art and others of a similar nature. Again, this special treatment is available only to foreigners. Although it is emphasised that there is political stability, politics can change and the laws can be revised – even in the United States. The advantage is the Americans would always grandfather new laws, allowing the foreign investor time to change their holdings. If one is located elsewhere, there is therefore the need for a professional advisor to be on the scene, or nearby and constantly reviewing the law to ensure their clients are protected. Although the US is used as an example, these are the considerations that must be made to evaluate all such zones.

Free trade zones also advertise privacy for financial statements and asset protection from expropriation by a foreign government or a foreign judgement. The problem is that financial statements must be filed and the US, for example, has frozen people's accounts and has the power to do so, even in the Montana zone. They advertise that they keep a staff of lawyers available to defend any action against accounts, another good feature. Other features to be looked at are the minimum size of any deposit (i.e. $200,000.00 for Montana) and the maximum that can be withdrawn without required documentation. In the US and Canada, any cash transfer or withdrawal of $10,000.00 (US) or more must be reported to the Government, and in Montana, any electronic transfer of $3,000.00 must be kept record of by the depository. Such would not be the case in most offshore centres, although they do have their own regulations as money laundering is of great concern to everyone. Other restrictions to watch for are restrictions on who can use the zone. For Montana the following are not allowed:

1. US citizens (even if they don't live in the US)
2. Resident Aliens
3. Any corporation if any shareholder (not all) is a citizen or resident
4. Any Trust if the settler (the person giving the assets to the Trust) or beneficiary is a citizen or resident
5. Any partnership if a member is a citizen or resident
6. Any person convicted of a felony in the US or any corporation where the controlling person has been convicted

These zones might have restrictions regarding the actual precious metal or other account allowed. Such restrictions might be that they must have a specified term to maturity for the account, and that it must terminate within a specified period. Other restrictions are penalties imposed for withdrawals before termination, limited withdrawal if allowed, especially if a debit card or credit card is used, special fees for such withdrawals, etc. Although income taxes might not be imposed, the cost of transacting business might nullify the effect. Another consideration is the possibility that taxes on dividend income or interest income from the financial institution might still be taxable in that jurisdiction, even though the increase in value due to growth might not be. For gold, the increasing value and the hedge against inflation might not be taxable, but if there is an element of interest income or dividend income attached to it, that might be taxable - a very tricky situation.

Confidentiality provisions of the Free Trade Zones are always suspect. Many protect the disclosure of financial records or statements. Such protection might not include a request by a court or government body, or even requirements of a tax treaty with another country, which is of concern. Such disclosure is only allowed when there is a suspicion of criminal activity, although it depends on the law in each zone. Many add the further protection of allowing a civil action against those who do get access improperly. Unfortunately, this is after the fact, and many tax or offshore travellers want to retain anonymity, thus such access defeats their intention and cannot be reversed once disclosed.

Offshore Centres that pose a possible threat

There are some islands and developing countries located around the world that pose an unseen threat to potential tax travellers. It is important that not only that favourable laws and conditions exist in an offshore, but that the tax traveller has looked at the history and potential risks on this status in the future. Many islands have a lower degree of business sophistication that goes hand in hand with a cultural remoteness, and although they have the laws in place, there are risks and threats that do not allow the usual benefits to be taken advantage of. Some of these states are so remotely located that they are virtually inaccessible by business. Some offshore countries have low taxes, yet they have a risk of a future change in their politics and economy imposed by, for example, a scheduled take-over by a major power. Hong Kong and Macau have had these problems with China, and although the Chinese have stated that the independent status the two former colonies possess shall remain unchallenged, the risk ominously remains.

Other centres were created as a result of a power-of-attorney declaration with the tribal owners of the country. This is the case for many of the South Pacific locations and, although run by strong businesspeople, there is a risk of change. For evaluating such locations, one must look at their track record and have strong assurances that the people of the island are committed to this status and are stable in their views. If a power-of-attorney declaration is made with a tribal chief who has a history of being in power and a long record of stability and ownership, there is a reduction of the risk. The Dominion of Melchizedek in the South Seas is one centre that is gaining in strength and is expanding its haven status dominion over other islands. This dominion is slowly reaching a level whereby it will have the confidence of the offshore community by establishing an acceptable level of credibility on an international scale. The benefit of this location is that its economy is not dependent on funding from a major power, so it is not susceptible to influence that could change their status. A definite positive condition and one that should be watched in the future as the major countries become more aggressive in their demands for exchange of information with countries that they have ties or influence over.

Unfortunately, there have been a number of fraudulent schemes associated with Melchizedek. Thus, in evaluating an offshore location, one must look at the history of fraudulent schemes and their validity before making a choice. The question is whether the past action is a good indication of what they would do in the future. Were these fraudulent schemes those that would impact on offshore activities? Are those people involved in the schemes still in power? Who are we dealing with? In Melchizedek, the president of the nation was allegedly involved in a fraud scheme regarding an insurance scam in the UK. An Austrian banker tried to cash a cheque for $500,000.00 and the US went after two Washington-based banks that weren't properly licensed in the US, yet they were licensed in Melchizedek. The country has since maintained that the criticism of their offshore operation is unfair and unwarranted, as that type of transaction was the work of individuals and that they had no control over them.

One should note that there could always be sham transactions in offshore locations, just as there will always be sham transactions in the US, Canada, the UK and Europe. Every country has a criminal element and those who break the law. In general, the existence of such activities is only an indication that proper scrutiny must be exercised, as there is a potential for problems. Also, even if the officials in the country and its offshore activities are proper, there might be difficulty for international commerce as a result of the bad image - a good reason, perhaps, not to be associated with such a location.

Yet another consideration in evaluating the choice of an offshore location is the influence of a major controlling country. In some instances, favourable laws are in place, yet there could be delays as a result of boundary disputes and ownership. For most island offshores this does not seem to be a problem, yet it can happen when there is only a special location on the Island where that status applies. Combined with the boundary consideration are the specialised laws of the offshore. If the offshore is set up for only certain types of entities that require location on the Island or within particular bounds of the offshore, then any boundary dispute can have serious ramifications. If there is a specialised zone, is control of the administrative requirements conducted from within or outside of the zone? If there is a specialised council that must approve the licensing, where is this specialised body located and how are the submissions and other documents submitted for approval protected? If those incorporating a business are to be active within the zone, is the location they are establishing in a possibly disputed area, what special requirements are imposed by the offshore in establishing the operation and during the ongoing activities of the offshore? What activities are given special treatment over other activities within the zone? What other special concessions can they take advantage of?

Other interesting relationships and arrangements can be used. Where there is a home country involved with an offshore, for example the Netherlands, can this country be used as a go-between to protect the confidentiality and create an appearance of a non-tax reason for the transaction? It might also be beneficial to be able to use a screen company in the home or main country with a conduit to the offshore centre. Some of the positive activities to look for in the offshore are within the areas of banking, insurance and industry. Other considerations are whether business can be conducted with residents and non-residents, non-residents without a permanent establishment, other zone entities, other non-zone entities and certain residents of the home country.

A Listing of Offshore Countries

There are many remote and developing offshore locations around the world. Many of them have been around for many years but have not been able to develop, as their lines of communication and business facilities are not at the level of current technological requirements. The new initiatives by major governments such as the US, UK and some European countries, and the locations they have ties with, will not stop tax haven activity. With the numerous offshore locations in the under-developed stage, a tightening of pressure by the powerful countries (US, UK, etc.) will only shift the activities from those offshore locations controlled by them to ones that are not controlled. The authorities would be better to leave things as they are and develop their own sites to try and capture the lucrative market that is increasing on a geometric scale.

Some of these potential future locations are:

1. The Canary Islands
2. Melchizedek
3. Norderfriedrichskoog
4. Svabald
5. Djibouti
6. North Korea
7. St. Barthelemy
8. United Arab Emirates
9. Oman
10. Hong Kong
11. Kiribati
12. Albania
13. Seychelles
14. Mauritius
15. Cook Islands
16. Marshall Islands
17. Bahrain
18. Pitcairn Island
19. Macau
20. New Caledonia
21. Enen-kio

These are in addition to the traditional tax havens that include:

1. Bahamas
2. Bermuda
3. British Virgin Islands (BVI)

4. Granada
5. Turks & Caicos
6. Cayman Islands
7. Netherlands Antilles
8. St. Vincent
9. Martinique
10. Costa Rica
11. Panama
12. Jersey (Channel Islands)
13. Guernsey (Channel Islands)
14. Isle of Man
15. Orkneys
16. Andorra
17. Liechtenstein
18. Switzerland
19. Greenland
20. Luxembourg
21. Monaco
22. Austria
23. Hong Kong
24. Singapore
25. Cyprus

The above list does not include all the offshore centres nor does it include the various trade zones. In fact, any country that provides an opportunity to reduce taxes can be considered a type of tax haven. With so many countries involved, it is better to join them than try to beat them.

Business & Market Conditions

Depending on the circumstances, the *no tax benefit* of an offshore country could be nullified by other taxes imposed locally. These taxes would have a greater impact if the offshore needed to locate part of their operation within the territory of the offshore. Bermuda is a prime example where high import duties are imposed. This could create a large increase in the cost of materials and other items that may need to be imported for use in manufacturing. These taxes also increase the costs of goods such as food and other necessities, making offshores such as Bermuda have a very high cost of living.

Other indirect taxes that are imposed by various countries are export duties, sales tax and stamp taxes. It is important to note that most offshore tax havens have low population figures and thus represent a small market from which a company would derive revenues. As a result, it is not normally advantageous to operate a business that will exist largely upon the revenue garnered in the haven location. In fact, many of these centres do not offer the special tax status on income derived locally, and others will not allow any domestic enterprise for special low tax status. Switzerland, for example, does not want a company to have more than 20 percent of its revenue derived from local sources. In other countries they merely provide the special tax status for revenue derived outside of that country. The offshore traveller must remember that low tax is not the only reason for using an offshore. For many, the protection of assets is of primary importance. Under this condition, the criteria for choosing an offshore location must be changed. Stability and protection of assets should be the dominant influence.

Others advocate that it is preferable to locate at a site where there may be some local market. This is due to the possibility of an emergency where the foreign base is restricted to external operations due to currency, expropriation, revolution, war or civil unrest. If there is any chance of such an event, the use of that country by the client could be highly restrictive in nature. One should also consider moving assets elsewhere and keeping a minimum locally. The use of the offshore as an intermediary company with no local assets would be the most desirable situation.

Many advisors believe that the more tax treaties an offshore has, the better. There is mixed feeling by tax professionals who are knowledgeable in this area. There are positive benefits as well as negative ones. The main negative factor is the maintenance of confidentiality. Although sometimes the treaty might guarantee confidentiality, dependence on trade as a result of a treaty could result in a future renegotiation of the treaty. An exchange of information is insisted upon and the non-tax haven party has gained significant bargaining position as a result of the increased dependence on trade. Thus, a treaty could represent a potential risk. Another consideration is, for example, the Barbados-Canada treaty, in that it provides for a low withholding tax rate on dividends paid from a Barbados company, or the other way around. Upon further scrutiny of the law, the tax traveller would find out that the benefits of the treaty are not available to a Barbados International Business Corporation (IBC). Appearances can thus be misleading and one needs to do close checking to ensure that a particular client qualifies for any favourable tax treatment as a result of a treaty.

Although one particular offshore might not be as beneficial as others currently, it might provide a potential future benefit. Using a tax haven in Europe might not be as beneficial as one of the offshore islands, yet there may be a future potential. With the advent of the European Union, locating in Switzerland or Liechtenstein could give access to a large domestic market, while maintaining special tax treatment. The benefit might be the reduction of tariffs and other restrictions while being in the centre of a strong market. Another location of similar benefit would be Costa Rica. The drawback is the potential that the haven raises its taxes as they become a more desirable location.

The long-term is one of the most important considerations for choosing an offshore tax haven. It is rare that an individual is looking for a short-term location, and this is especially true for larger corporations. The question is how long will the special tax status survive. It is always a risk that a new government will change the law. Comfort can be derived from the fact that if a country prospers as a low tax country, it is unlikely that a new government would risk economic problems by changing the laws significantly. The offshore country must be solid as a financial centre with a strong commitment to the continuance of the current tax structure. Many companies have benefited from the use of offshores in the long-term by increasing their profitability through the reduction of taxes, normally achieved by separating the profits from a location into a separate company, using an offshore centre as an operational centre. The benefit of such use is that even if revenues or pre-tax profits decline, the after-tax profits can show a steady increase. This is solid financial management and has resulted in the increase in the value of many a company's profitability and market rating.

Another consideration to a company looking to locate offshore is the ability of the offshore country to control inflation internally. If the country is experiencing rapid inflation, and the cost of living is rapidly increasing, they are certainly not as desirable a location for companies. A strong credit policy is also important, since without one, the local financial industry could suffer major setbacks resulting in a major or minor collapse of banking. This could jeopardise the assets of those individuals and others who have assets locally and have a good credit rating.

To attract larger businesses, an offshore country must have the ability to generate capital when required. Companies are always in need of capital and if there is a strong base for obtaining the capital, it will encourage foreign-based companies to locate there. The existence of major recognised commercial institutions can make or break the desirability of an offshore. This has been the secret of Switzerland, as it has a massive holding of hard currency. The maintenance of bank secrecy is also a major influence. If they loosen their policy on secrecy, it will hurt their financial position.

Considerations for Conducting Business

There are various approaches to conducting business in an offshore location. One is actually conducting the full operation within the offshore. This requires a full complement of qualified people for the required jobs, availability of equipment and machinery, ability to import goods for raw materials and fixed assets, the ability to export goods, professional services, banking, capital availability and a dependable workforce. Another approach is to conduct the main head office administrative functions at the offshore. This would require qualified personnel as well, including qualified office personnel, senior management, professional advisors, communications and all the necessary conditions to do international business.

From the above brief analysis it can be seen that the preliminary consideration is the evaluation of the workforce availability. Are there qualified office personnel such as secretarial help, clerks, an acceptable level of literacy and the ability to handle confidential information? Some do not consider the confidentiality of clerical personnel important, yet once set up in some offshore countries companies have found that they could not find personnel that they could trust with performing confidential duties with efficiency and the maintenance of secrecy. The IRS, in some of its sting operations, used this fact to place personnel at strategic locations where offshore staff frequented, to gather information about the taxpayer. It is indeed puzzling that companies located in the US have information that is top secret, and value that secrecy so religiously, yet sometimes they allow such discretion to be forgotten when dealing with their offshore matters.

Regarding the labour force, if people have to be trained, there is the cost of training as well as the size of the workforce. In some locations, although there is a skilled work force, they may be less than reliable due to adverse conditions, or their work standard, sometimes culturally-based, might not be compatible to that existing in the client's home base state. These people have had to employ and train twice the normal workforce to ensure there was a proper backup of personnel, otherwise they would have slowdowns and lose business. As the number of persons who are employed is increased, so is the likelihood of a leak of information. Sometimes a company will decide to bring in their own labour force. Living conditions and costs of accommodation became a major factor in the equation when that occurs. Personnel from other countries would require a specific standard of living, availability of recreational facilities, medical, schools and even communication with their home base. The costs to provide an imported labour force could far outweigh the savings. Some companies have therefore set up their operation in two or three locations, designing the structure to take advantage of the availability of various components in each country.

The geographic location of the offshore and its proximity to markets and other factors can be essential. Even though raw materials might not have heavy duties attached to them, if they are too far away, there will be delays in transportation and higher costs of transportation. There might even be limitations on the mode of transportation and higher risk factors for certain modes. Is the offshore on a major shipping route and how often do ships, etc., come to that port? Special shipments are always more costly and cut in to profit margins. The process of production requires power. What power facilities are available at the offshore, how costly are they, and can the offshore service the required level of usage without a strain on their system? The best offshore tax haven is one where management is closer to the scene of the operation. The scene of a company's operation includes the market to which it caters to. A business should consider several locations if it operates in specific areas of the world.

Another consideration is incorporation and other laws within a country. It can be difficult to do business where the laws are difficult for management. That is, the liability of managers regarding what they do for the corporation is not satisfactory. The laws could make them personally liable for all actions, even if done on behalf of the corporation. Others do not separate the distinction between domestic and foreign operations. The preservation of autonomy for foreign operations can be very important and if this cannot be done due to foreign laws, a company might be forced to look elsewhere. It is very important to analyse all corporate laws before deciding. Corporate considerations include banking, types of shares, procedure for incorporation, application requirements, shareholder requirements, director requirements, minimum capital and statutory requirements for a local representative.

Obviously, the more liberal and discretionary the laws, the better they are for flexibility in planning purposes. As more and more information is being pursued by major powers, disclosure requirements of the local government become a major consideration. If the government has a treaty with the US, as an example, that requires access to information available to the government, the requirements are very important. A government that requires no disclosure of information from corporations or shareholders has nothing to give to another country where it has an exchange of information agreement. Another interesting consideration is the language used. It is very difficult to do business if the local language used is not spoken by any of the company officers or owners. The language spoken at the market where the company operates should be the same as that used where they have set up shop.

Security of Assets

The success of a company in a tax haven can be totally nullified if the government has a history of expropriation of assets without any regard for local contract and other law. It is for this reason that many companies operating through a tax haven do not leave their assets located in that country. The local government must uphold its contract law as stated (the law must also be solid and reliable for protection of rights), as well as have strong laws for the protection of property. The law must have provision for compensation that is adequate in the case of a violation of such rights by anyone, including the government. Does the government have a high regard for the rights of foreigners, including the treatment of royalty or license agreements? The country should have a strong reputation regarding credit, to allow a company to compete internationally. Without this assurance, international financial institutions will not do business with them.

CHAPTER 3
SOME ASPECTS OF
INTERNATIONAL LAW

To really understand the benefits of offshore tax havens, and how to make choices, the professional and user must understand some of the basics of international law. International law is made up of a system of principles and rules that govern the relationships between sovereign states, as well as with transnational bodies. It focuses primarily on those rules that exist between specific states or as means of governing the relations of international organisations to which individual states are members. These rules encompass nearly all state-to-state activities, from use of the seas to that of outer space, and from transfer of money to international trade, security and communications.

The authority by which international law is based upon stems from the reality that the international community recognises and accepts to be bound by a specific set of international agreements and treaties as law. Like national law, international law has reasonably clear sources of law – those that are law-creating and law-identifying. Despite an absence of the kind of formal institutions that create domestic within a state, there are established methods for the creation of legal rules and different ways in which the exact content of those laws can be identified.

Creation and Ascertaining International Law: Sources of Law

Article 38 of the Statute of the International Court of Justice

Article 38 of the Statute of the ICJ is present international law. The Statute of the Court (on creating the court) states the court's functions, hierarchy and states how the court should decide a case and what court is entitled to rely upon the decision.

Article 38 is a codification of customary international law:

- hierarchy, as far as listing what terms shall apply
- international conventions (treaties)
- international custom, as evidence of general practice accepted
- general principles of law (as recognised by civilised nations)
- judicial decisions are material sources but don't create law (the decision of the ICJ has a *de facto* approach)

This *hierarchy* is important at a theoretical level, but less so at the practical level and refers to the process of law creation and identification in finding the law. Article 38 itself does not outline hierarchy and there are often conflicts that can be resolved by interpreting the rules. The same rule may be derived from more than one of the law-creating processes (i.e. law-making treaties that are codifications of custom).

Soft Law is a term from the 1970s, used for *lex ferenda* (law-developing - not yet law). It is relevant because of the custom and how it evolves, an example being the Regime of the Continental Shelf. In 1945, offshore oil was discovered in what is now known as the Continental Shelf, US President Truman claiming ownership. Other countries also made claims that led to assertion of rights to the shelf, as did questions over the so-called *3-mile limit* off shore. By 1949, the Continental Shelf was established *lex lata,* which is considered black letter law, or Hard Law.

Soft law is sometimes used to describe areas within the laws of Human Rights and that of the environment. The norms are agreed upon, but final considerations and definitions are not yet decided, yet the general norms enjoy some basic agreement. It can be said that soft law really describes the law that is *law,* but has not been flushed out enough so that it is enforceable and has not yet become a legal principle.

Treaties

The first source of law, as outlined by Article 38 of the ICJ, is that found in treaties. Treaties are used as a tool to create law, and this binding of international norms is relatively new. There is no distinction made in Article 38 as to types of treaties. Treaties that are bilateral in nature (*treates contrats)* are contractual in scope and don't purport to establish international law norms. (i.e. the 1867 Treaty of Friendship, Commerce and Navigation between Japan and Denmark). *Traites-lois* are treaties of a law-creating nature and most treaties negotiated in the 20th century are of this type.

Treaties as a source of law have been questioned, but they are distinct and important, i.e. The UN Charter, which sets out norms that go beyond the contracting parties. Also for consideration would be the 1982 Law of the Sea Convention, those pertaining to human rights, and the Geneva Conventions. The treaty can be seen as both a contract and as a source of law. As in the law of contract found in domestic law, treaties create specific obligations that must be obeyed, and this is a rule of customary international law found in the legal maxim *pacta sunt servanda*. Like a contract, this customary law dictates that states must fulfil their treaty obligations, though according to this principle the specific terms within the treaty are not law, but legal obligations. Yet, a treaty can also be said to be a source of law in that the state is bound by the terms of a treaty, therefore it is legally bound to act in a particular manner, thus it has created law for it is bound by. It does this by regulating the future actions of the parties to the letter of the treaty; this in effect makes the treaty a source of law.

Negotiations of Treaties: the Process and the Effect

The laws governing that of peace and war were developed by custom and are currently regulated exclusively by treaty because there has been a change in the terms of instruments of international law. The diverse interests of states makes it harder to get customary rules by state agreement. Also, there have been vast technological changes, such as that of air flight and new weaponry, rendering previous customary law obsolete and requiring new treaties.

The Law of the Sea developed through custom. There were diverse interests in such matters as that of the Continental Shelf and the exploitation of such. Some of the fisheries were mass factory ships on the high seas and states were asserting jurisdiction onto the high seas and beyond the Continental Shelf. Without the conclusion and reliance of a treaty, control is based on custom.

Some examples of Treaties are:

- UNCLOS III (Law of the Sea), negotiated between 1970-1982, and came into force in 1994 (25 years after negotiations began). The treaty was created out of thin air. Even in the 1970s there were exclusive economic zones that were treated as law based on the negotiations that were on-going, so therefore before the conclusion of the treaty, the process had generated a norm of customary law.

- SALT II negotiations (strategic arms limitations) were never ratified by the US Congress, but they have abided by the terms of the treaty, despite the fact it has not become law.

Negotiations of treaties can have an enormous effect on international law and how states behave.

What is a Treaty?

- need two parties who are internationally recognised as having the capacity to enter into a treaty (usually states, but can also be international organisations).
- they agree on something (more than a contract, i.e. a loan agreement between two countries, which would be enforced by private law rather than public international law). Treaties are governed by public international law and not private law.
- the parties must have the intention to create a binding agreement.

The Rules for treaty-making are set out in the *Vienna Convention* (passed in 1969 and came into force in 1980), which codifies much of the customary law of treaties, and it applies to treaties concluded after 1980. The Vienna Convention is referred to in assisting with interpretation of treaties. Oral treaties are possible, but the Vienna Convention doesn't refer to them (i.e. nuclear test cases – a statement can be taken as a unilateral treaty – but the Vienna Convention only applies to treaties between states).

The Vienna Convention includes

Art. 1 - only applies to treaties between states

Art. 2 - treaty must be between states and in written form for the purpose of this convention

Art. 3 - only applies to parties to the Vienna Convention itself. Agreements not between states or not in written form are not covered by the convention, but are still binding under customary law

Art. 5 - the convention applies to any treaty that is the constituent instrument of an international organisation

Art. 6 - every state possesses the capacity to conclude treaties – the authority of municipal governments depends upon the purpose of a treaty prior to its entry into force.

The intention of the parties to create binding relations under international law, and the fact that the agreement is governed by international law, are essential elements (i.e. a mere state organisation or singular arm of government likely does not have the ability to conclude a treaty).

Some agreements may just be voluntary economic restraints in order to circumvent a treaty, i.e. Japan negotiating to limit shipments of Toyotas or the 1908 agreements between the US and Japan that modified normal immigration requirements where Japanese were made so-called *honorary Caucasians*. Therefore, some instruments are clearly not binding, and sometimes there is ambiguity intentionally.

To find out whether or not agreements are intended to be governed by international law, look at

- intention: to be binding, use of *will* or *shall*
- memorandums of understanding; precise undertakings with a clear understanding that they are not to be binding - estoppel argument (vagueness goes to intent- remember, over time soft law can become hard law)
- subsequent actions of the parties - compliance over time
- is the agreement registered under Article 102 of the United Nations Charter (some are not registered - not binding treaty)
- who has signed the agreement? A representative with full powers?

Practical implications: from non-treaties

1. legal implications: the doctrine of estoppel is a principle of international law, if the treaty is binding (estoppel is a legal rule of evidence precluding one party from denying the truth of a statement, stated or written, made by that party of the existence of facts, whether existing or not, which that party by words or conduct led another to believe in);
2. assertion of jurisdiction, i.e. Spain going to international court to fight Canada for apprehending a fishing vessel on the high seas (Canada did not agree to the international court's jurisdiction re: Canada's fishing legislation). Both Canada and Spain are members of the international court but Canada had a reservation;

Technical aspects of treaty-making

There are steps for entering into a treaty and codification of customary international law. The Vienna Convention changes the way treaties are concluded and therefore the nature of the treaty has changed.

Someone must negotiate, such as an ambassador, to conclude a treaty. The nature of the communications must be specific about what would be negotiated, given a document specifying the details, precise terms, and limits of authority. This is called *Full Powers* and they give the consent of the state. Historically, the ambassador would have full powers, so ratification by the state is just a formality. The representative will probably have powers to allow negotiations, adopt text, offer their signature, but not treaty ratification. Most treaties consist of a letter with a line for a signature, and there is an exchange of notes which is binding on signature or at a time specified. There is no formal ratification required, and many appear just to be housekeeping issues today (i.e. whether or not we respect driving licenses, or minor immigration formalities, etc.). Article 7(2) is implicit that authentication of a treaty is only with consent of the state, through the intentions of the person representing the state.

Article 9 instructs that adoption is by the consent of all states participating; multilateral treaty-making ends with agreement on adoption of the text by unanimous agreement. There is a need to recognise that if a veto is allowed, then some states will deliberately sabotage the vote- inhibiting rule (especially if there are 125 states around the table). A bilateral treaty must have unanimity and a multilateral can disagree at the adoption stage.

There is no required procedure as to how consent by states to treaties is expressed. Differing ways that states express consent are:

- ratification
- acceptance
- approval

Treaties are subject to ratification by their state, and in most cases this allows for consideration of the political implications of the treaty in question. As examples, in the US treaties must be ratified by the Senate, whereas in Canada treaties are ratified by the Crown (Governor-General) after acceptance by Parliament. The act of ratification is universally required by the states themselves (not by international law).

In some instances, states that were not party to a treaty when it was first created can come aboard after the fact. This has considerable implications for offshores, as a tax haven may enter into a treaty years after the treaty was first introduced, creating new legal implications. The state must first take three steps:

1. adopt the text of the treaty
2. authenticate the treaty itself
3. open the treaty for proper signatures (by heads of state)

The state then turns over the instrument to the Secretary General of the United Nations, where a strict procedure is followed. There is an obligation not to defeat the object and purpose of a treaty prior to its entry into force. So, if a state signed a treaty that is not yet in force, there are obligations under international law (note that a state is not bound under Art. 18 to carry out the treaty, but must refrain from acts that will defeat the object and purpose of the treaty).Treaties have wide implications on almost every consideration of tax havens, and although a Herculean task, it is in the best interest of the professional and client to make themselves familiar with the mechanisms of treaties, the treaties that bind the home country of the tax traveller, and the treaties that bind the tax haven state. Examples and test problems related to treaties and international law are found in Appendix B.

CHAPTER 4
BASICS OF U.S. TAX LAW RE: OFFSHORE OPERATIONS

As early as 1986, the US imposed legislation as well as yearly changes to the tax laws directed towards foreign corporations and individuals doing business in the US and abroad. These provisions initially attempted to place foreign corporations doing business through a branch in the same tax position as foreign corporations that do business through a US subsidiary. Congress intended the law to override existing treaties in an effort to prevent foreign corporations rotating taxes by treaty shopping, establishing branches in country subdivisions or reducing taxes imposed on these corporate subsidiaries. Many Americans still believe that foreign corporations have a tax advantage over domestic corporations and the country needs to protect itself from such investors. Whether these beliefs are well founded or not, their existence has not been ignored and revenue officials have been constantly on the look out for ways to control taxation of foreign business investments.

The internal revenue code currently imposes a maximum rate of 39.6 percent on individuals. This rate and the next lower rate of 36 percent exceed the amount of tax imposed on non-resident individuals of 35 percent. However, one must understand that the rate imposed on foreigners of 35 percent does not allow deductions that are available to the local people. As a result, foreigners might or might not be taxed at a higher rate. In the US, the definition of resident versus non-resident is significant in determining a tax treatment of individuals as well as other entities. The Internal Revenue Code contains many provisions that are directed towards a *US person*, defined in the Code as "a citizen or resident of the United States, the domestic partnership, the domestic corporation, and any Estate or Trust". An Estate or Trust is an organisation that has income "from sources without the United States which is not effectively connected with the conduct of a trading business within the United States". The Code clearly distinguishes between individuals and other entities. The test for residency for corporations and other entities continues to be unclear and could be an area of conflict between the Internal Revenue Service and the foreign investor. Currently, the Internal Revenue Service, with support from the courts, looks at the facts and circumstances to determine the definition. This accords the Internal Revenue Service a great deal of discretion, although it also opens up the opportunity for challenge in the courts; the problem is that one does not want to have to go to court to solve the issue.

Any individual who is not a US citizen is only considered a resident if they meet two conditions. That individual must be lawfully admitted for permanent residence, or meet something called the substantial presence test. The substantial presence test requires residency in the United States for 183 days in the current year, or at least 31 days during the current account year - at least 183 days of residency as determined under a weighted average formula. The actual number of days in the current year plus one-third of the days in the first proceeding year plus 160 days in the second preceding year, is what constitutes the substantial presence test. This provision disallows any day an individual was in the US as a diplomat, full-time employee of an international organisation, member of family of the preceding individuals, a teacher, trainee, a student, or professional athlete present for a charitable sports event. Any individual who commutes from Canada or Mexico or was in transit between two foreign destinations and is in the US for less than 24 hours is not considered a resident for the day. These tests can also be satisfied if you have a tax home in a foreign country, or had a closer connection to a foreign home and maintain significant contacts in the foreign country. This combined with being in the US less than 183 days during the year would defeat the presence test. In addition, many of the treaties the US has signed have special rules for determining residency where laws of both countries treat that particular individual as a resident. That is, if there is a conflict of laws.

For corporations, the Internal Revenue Service takes the position that a corporation formed on the laws of any state is considered domestic. The problem is when does the foreign corporation obtain US residence. The corporation is considered resident if it is engaged in a trade business within the US, unless it has foreign income that is not effectively connected with a trade or business within the United States. Before a foreign corporation can have any effectively connected income, it must be determined that it is engaged in trade or business within the US.

Residency status of a Trust or Estate can affect the US taxation as well as taxation regarding the beneficiaries of the Trust. A Trust established under US law is considered a US resident and subject to the same rules as any citizen. If the Trust is formed under a foreign country's laws, the status of that Trust for tax purposes is affected by several factors. As used in most legislation, the internal code definition of foreign Trusts uses a negative definition. That is, the definition defines what is not a foreign Trust. For example, a Trust that is not subject to US tax on its world-wide income is considered foreign. The definition focuses on the facts around the Trust that allows the Internal Revenue Service discretion and the courts to provide guidance in this area. In effect, this allows a degree of discretion so that the courts and the Internal Revenue Service can narrow or broaden the definition. The Internal Revenue Service has issued a ruling that narrows considerably the requirements further than those established in previous case law. This ruling was from 1973, where the existence of a US Trustee is deemed sufficient to classify the Trust as domestic.

The determination of the status of an Estate for Estate tax purposes, or non-resident, is generally based on the domicile (normally permit residents) of the individual at the time of the death. A non-resident who purchases or leases property in the United States, and shows an intention to make it their domicile, is considered as having created a domicile in the US. This is true even if the individual is not present in the US at the time of death. For the situation where the deceased person did not have a US domicile, the taxation of the Estate can be affected by the actions of the Executor or the nature of the Estate property. The existence of a US Executor who actively manages the assets of the Estate may be sufficient to subject the Estate to residency status and tax it on its world-wide income.

The US Internal Revenue Code does not specifically define a corporation. The term *corporation* includes an association, insurance company and a joint stock company. At one time the Internal Revenue Code required officials to look at the definition from a negative point of view and from this approach, and the common law, six characteristics were developed to determine whether it is a corporation. These characteristics are:

- Associates
- Objective to carry on business and divide profits
- Continuity of life
- Centralised management
- Limited liability
- The transferability of interest.

The Internal Revenue Code defines a partnership as a joint venture or other unincorporated organisation to which a business venture is carried on. It goes further to say that a partnership is not a corporation, Trust or Estate for tax purposes. The domestic partnership is one that is organised or created under US law. The basic law makes a partnership identical to a US person. Foreign and domestic partnerships are both subject to withholding tax where distribution is to a foreign entity. This foreign entity must be deemed to be from income "effectively connected" and was from the trade or business within the US. The rates established are the highest rate of tax imposed on the foreign entity. This amount is to be paid by the partnership according to regulations and is treated as a deemed distribution on all amounts provided by the regulations. Quarterly payments are normally required.

Most states have what is called the *limited liability company*. It is speculated that the Internal Revenue Service in determination of a limited liability corporation (LLC) looks to the definition of a corporation. If an entity is not a corporation it potentially can be considered as being a limited liability corporation. This type of corporation is limited by statute regarding transferability of interests, termination on the death retirement, or bankruptcy of any member. Many states however do allow transferability when all members approve. Thus, the limited liability corporation is similar to a partnership.

In the US, a Trust includes those created by will as well as those *inter vivos* Trusts or those created while people are still alive. The six tests cited for incorporation are also used to determine whether a Trust exists. The individual that grants a Trust should not be the administrator of the Trust, or its existence will be ignored for federal tax purposes. A Trust normally has a fixed life, term certain, or special conditions for certain events. Failure to set these conditions or any other conditions could result in the Trust being treated as a corporation. The

99

existence of the Trustee can be viewed as centralized management and if there is any appearance of being an active business, the Trust could be considered to be a corporation. Any Trust which is not "effectively connected" with a trade or business is considered an alien for US taxation purposes. Estates and Trusts created through the death of a taxpayer states that a non-resident is subject to some sort of transfer tax on property owner at the time of death where it is located in the US.

The Key Elements for Consideration

Trade or Business

A foreign entity must have an office or other fixed place of business within the US. Under certain conditions the use of a US agent creates or replaces a place of business. Under most treaties with the US, the existence of a fixed facility creates a permanent establishment if the foreign entity is carrying on commercial or industrial activity. To be fixed, a place must be located at the distinct deemed geographical place where a taxpayer consistently conducts their activities. The space may or may not be rented. This would include space rented for a trade show that was of a short duration. The facility where activities are exclusively conducted on behalf of a foreign operation could also be considered a permanent establishment. Exceptions to this rule would be purchasing agents, or any information gathering activities for advertising entities. These activities must be conducted exclusively for the foreign entity to be excluded. Thus activities conducted through independent agents with authority to contract, or that eventually does contract on its own behalf, could result in a permanent residence. This approach is also taken in treaties between the US and Canada, and trade treaties between the US and the UK. The agency relationship requirement is not necessarily strictly a legal one, but is based more on the facts and circumstances of each case. US law has been known to recognise the parent subsidiary, consignor-consignee, or company and commission agent relationship as an agency one. It should be noted that even if a permanent establishment is determined, the agent must be dependent.

In parent subsidiary relationships, there is not a presumption of the dependent agent. This means that just because the two entities are related doesn't automatically mean that there is a dependant agent. In such a case, the subsidiary will be subject to tax on US income unless the substance is considered dependent. The IRS would have an argument that it is dependent if the subsidiary is 100 percent owned. Common law illustrates that in the US they would also have to show that there is an exclusive distributorship that has no control over prices and selling activities.

In a consignor-consignee relationship the entities are normally not at risk of being taxed. One must be very careful in such a relationship, to insure the consignor does not retain any risks and controls. The IRS has issued several rulings in this area. It is important to examine US law to determine if one is an employee or an independent contractor. The consignee-consignor or any commission agent case can be argued using these rules. This argument came about when used by the Internal Revenue Service in previous arguments regarding foreign insurance companies doing business through a US agent corporation. If one looks at the whole situation, it is a matter of control. Are they truly under the control of someone that could be called an employer? Another consideration is the element of risk of loss by the agent. The foreign entity should not assume the risk of loss for the goods in the agent's control. The absence of this economic risk with other factors could be very persuasive to a court that a dependent relationship exists.

Being effectively connected is determined by applying two tests. The first test uses the assets, whereas the second looks at business activities. That is, it looks to the income that is generated by particular assets in the US business. Regarding business activities, the Internal Revenue Service looks to whether the entity accounts for non-US income. If income is determined as being effectively connected, any individual who is a member of the foreign partnership will also be considered to have effectively connected income. This does not include capital gains, portfolio interest, or other specialised types of income. A similar rule is used for Estates and Trusts.

The term *Carry on Business* can be derived from any tax treaty and is normally defined using the facts and circumstances. Since it is a matter of fact and circumstances, contribution of assets could be sufficient to create this notion. This is one of the most difficult concepts to determine in advance. Other criteria relate to the continuity of life. An organisation will not be found to have met this test if the death, retirement, or bankruptcy of a member will cause the organisation to cease operations. This test is similar to a normal partnership.

Centralised management looks to the concentration of operating decisions and major policy decisions made by a limited group of individuals that may or may not be owners. At times this test is referred to as the mind and management rule. In situations where the true residence of a corporation is hard to determine, this test wood look to where the decisions of upper management are actually being made. For Trusts, the power of the Trustee is to manage the assets and conduct business on behalf of the Trust. Last, it is only logical that the location of the Trust under US law would be where the Trustee is exerting control.

The US Internal Revenue Code describes gross income as income from whatever source derived. The Code specifically excludes interest in certain state and municipal bonds, although, under the alternative tax method, such income might be taxed. There are several categories of income resulting in different tax treatment, as well as different treatments regarding prevention of losses and offset of gains. The Code also describes capital assets as all properties, except five specific categories. Any gain or loss from the sale of a capital assets is considered either short-term

or long-term. Gains and losses from capital assets are netted. The net amount for a period is included in income. The maximum rate on net capital gains is 28 percent. Short-term gains are taxed at mirror rates, while net losses that are in excess of the gains can be deducted to the amount of $3000.00 (US) per year against other sources of income. Short-term losses must be deducted first, and then long-term losses. Any non-deducted losses can be for carried forward to future years. Income is divided into one of three groups: passive, portfolio or active. Passive income expenses and credits from investments must be netted. A net passive loss must be carried forward until the investment generates passive income or it is sold. Passive activities are defined as any trade or business which the taxpayer does not materially participate in for that year, or any rental activity without regard to participation by the taxpayer. What constitutes material participation was not given in the statute. The regulations provide a series of seven tests used to determine if material participation has occurred:

1. more than 500 hours during the year;
2. the activity constitutes substantially all the participation in the activity;
3. participates more than 100 hours and this amount does not exceed any other participants' activity during year;

4. participation in all activities exceeds 500 hours, except it does not exceed 500 hours for any one activity;
5. the material participation test is met in at least five of any ten proceeding tax years;
6. the activity is a service activity in which the taxpayer participated in three of any proceeding tax years;
7. based on facts and circumstances the taxpayer's participation is regular, continuous, and substantial.

Such passive loss provisions defined, an interest by an individual in a limited partnership has a passive activity and indicates specifically that it cannot be considered active. The code does allow a deduction for active participation in Real Estate property if it meets the test established by the Code. The amount of additional losses allowed is $25,000.00 per year. The $25,000.00 is limited by 50 percent of an individual's gross income for the year that exceeds $100,000.00. Active participation does not involve the same level of participation as material participation. If an individual participates in determining whether major renovations are made to the property, and possibly helps to select a management company, it qualifies as active participation.

The amount of losses allowed for passive income decreases in each year. The losses allowed must then be used against portfolio income before losses can be offset against active income. Any passive loss that cannot be used is held until the investment is either sold or until income is generated. The regulations provide a formula for allocating such suspended losses where more than one passive activity occurs. Portfolio income is also segregated, and losses in excess of portfolio income cannot be deducted against active income.

Active income includes income from rendering services, profit from a trade or business in which a taxpayer is a material participant, a gain or loss of the sale of assets used in active trade or business, and income from intangible property where the taxpayer's personal efforts contributed to the creation of the property. Active income is not limited in that allowable losses from the other forms of income can be offset against active income. Deductions are traditionally allowed against income. There are two main categories of deductions: those for adjusted gross income and those from adjusted gross income. The documents for adjusted gross income include ordinary and necessary business expenses, reimbursed employee expenses, losses from sale or exchange of business property, expenditures for the production of income, penalties for early withdrawal from bank accounts and alimony. The code allows a taxpayer to select from two approaches in determining the amount adopted from adjusted gross income. One option is the fixed amount based on the taxpayer's status (i.e. single, married, etc.). This amount is adjusted each year for inflation. The second option is to itemise deductions. Such deductions are itemised as follows:

1. medical deductions
2. taxes
3. interest
4. charitable contributions
5. miscellaneous deductions.

There are certain other exemptions specified that the taxpayer may deduct related to the number of taxpayers within the tax unit. That is, taxpayers are granted one exemption for themselves, their spouse and each of their dependants.

The current provisions for taxation replaced personal exemptions and reduce the listed deductions for taxpayers with income above a certain amount. Personal exemptions are reduced by two percent for every $2500.00 of income, or fraction thereof, of that income exceeding specified levels. The itemised deductions are reduced by three percent of the amount of income that is in excess of the specified floor or 80 percent. These amounts are adjusted yearly based on inflation. Individuals may use several accounting methods in determining income, but traditionally individuals use the cash method of accounting. For trade or business and other income producing activities, the taxpayer may elect to use an accrual or modified cash basis. The IRS has the option of changing a taxpayer's accounting system if it can be demonstrated that the new methods more clearly reflect income and deductions.

The US taxes its citizens on world-wide income regardless of being outside the scope of its many treaty agreements. Individuals earning income from foreign sources have three provisions to allow them to avoid double taxation on earnings. First, the taxpayer can take a deduction for the foreign taxes paid. Second, the taxpayer can use the taxes as a credit instead of a deduction. The amount of a credit to be used against taxes is the lesser of the foreign taxes paid or an overall limitation. That overall limitation is determined by dividing combined taxpayer's income before personal and dependency exemptions and multiplying that amount by the US tax. The third option available is to exclude a specified amount of foreign income. In order to qualify for this option, a taxpayer must demonstrate that they meet the to test for bona fide residency, or meet the test of being physically present for an estimated minimum of 330 days within any 12 consecutive months. The taxpayer must be stationed outside the US for at least one year or, otherwise the IRS will contend the taxpayer's work was temporary and not allow the exclusion. This excluded amount is $70,000.00. This amount is only allowed if the taxpayer was present in the foreign country for all 365 days. The exclusion is reduced by the ratio of the number of days in the foreign country over

365. If the exclusion is elected, it is in effect until actively revoked. When revoked, that revocation is in effect for four more years. Thus, it is prudent, that the taxpayer examine each alternative carefully in relation to their intended location before they make a decision. In addition to the income exclusion, the US also grants a reduction of income for living expenses in excess of the base amount. This base amount is set at 16 percent of the income paid as a specified level. These elections, credits and exclusions must be made when the return is filed. As such, the filing date is extended to 15th June, with an automatic extension to 15th August.

Domestic Corporations

Treatment of Corporations is consistent with the taxation of individuals. Income from capital transactions uses the same rules as individuals. Net capital gains are taxed as ordinary income, corporations are not allowed capital losses in excess of capital gains. These laws are similar to those in Canada as a matter of interest. Unused capital losses are carried back three years and carried forward five years to offset capital gains. All corporate capital loss carry backs and carry forwards are treated as short-term.

Corporations also have special treatment for dividend income. A corporation can deduct 100 percent of dividends received from a domestic corporation which is a non-consolidated affiliate of which 80 percent or more is owned by the corporate entity. For corporations owning 20 to 80 percent, the dividend deduction for the dividend received is limited to 80 percent. For corporations owning less than 20 percent, the deduction is limited to 70 percent. The amount of the deduction is subject to a limit. This limit is determined by multiplying taxable income before dividends, the net operating loss deduction, and any loss carry back by the deduction percentage as determined by the level of ownership. The limit is not applied when the corporation has a net operating loss.

The rate of tax for a corporation is a graduated tax with an initial rate of 15 percent for income up to $50,000.00, 25 percent for income from $50,001.00 to $75,000.00, 34 percent for income from $75,001.00 to $100,000.00. When earnings exceed $100,000.00, a surtax is imposed on the income above $100,000.00 at 3 percent to a level of $335,000.00. Once corporate income exceeds 10 million, the rate is increased to 35 percent. Another three percent surtax is added when corporate income exceeds $15 million. This 38 percent rate applies to income up to $18,333,003.00 and effectively taxes all income earned to this level at a flat rate of 35 percent. Income above this amount is taxed at a 35 percent rate. It should be noted that these rates are not permitted for personal service corporations, which applies a 35 percent rate on all income. The personal service corporation is one that is substantially employee owned and whose principal activities are the performance of services such as health, law, engineering, architecture, accounting, actuarial science, performing arts, or consulting fields. The graduated rates are also denied any related corporations.

Foreign Income

Special provisions for corporations having income are included in the Internal Revenue Code. Corporations are allowed to take a credit or deduction for foreign taxes deemed paid or accrued. In order to qualify deductible taxes must be those directly assessed on the corporation or those paid indirectly through a subsidiary or branch. The corporation must have an ownership interest of at least 10 percent in the foreign subsidiary. The ownership interest of 10 percent applies not only at the first tier operation, but also a 10 percent overall ownership rule must be satisfied and 5 percent direct ownership rules also are met. The foreign tax imposed on a lower tier can also be passed to the upper tier.

These limitations were enacted to avoid double taxation of foreign income. US corporations were using the credit provisions established by these rules to shelter other types of income that were taxed at lower rates. Congress decided to separate the different types of income into five categories to establish limitations. They eliminated the separate limitation on passive interest income and replaced it with a limitation on all passive income. The definition for passive income is essentially that imposed under the foreign personal holding company provisions. Passive income as one could imagine, includes dividends, interest annuities, and certain rents and royalties. Income from the sale of non-income producing property that gives the risk to a personal holding company will also be classified as passive.

The second income category is dividends received from each corporation where ownership is between 10 and 50 percent of the voting power or stock value. The third category is interest income subject to a foreign withholding tax of at least five percent. Income from the active conduct of a banking or financial business or certain types of insurance company or other financial services is the fourth category. Shipping income is the fifth category. The rules require that if a particular category has losses, those losses are allocated among the other categories and any excess can then be used to reduce US income. In addition to these categories, separate limitations are imposed on income from domestic international sales corporations or foreign sales corporations and foreign trade income. Any unused foreign credit can be carried back two years and forward five years within its respective category.

Besides the separation of income into categories, the available foreign tax credit is adjusted for foreign net operating losses deducted in previous periods. The foreign tax credit is reduced by the lower of remaining non-recaptured foreign losses, or 50 percent of foreign source income, until losses have been recaptured. Where non-recaptured foreign losses exist and the US taxpayer disposes of trade or business property used predominantly outside the US, the taxpayer has US source income to the extent of the lesser of the gain on disposition or the remaining loss.

Partnerships

Tax is not imposed on earnings of a partnership at the partnership level. They are treated as conduits with respect to income and deductions. The income is actually taxed at the individual level. Several types of elections under the Code are made at the partnership level. There can be an election to expense rather than appreciated equipment, which must be made by the partnership and designated on the forms provided to the partners. Partners are subject to tax on earnings of the partnership that has a foreign source.

For tax years after 1997, if the partnership has any effectively connected taxable income for any year that is allocable to a foreign partner, the partnership must withhold tax. The amount of withholding tax is the highest applicable rate, 39.6 percent for individuals and 35 percent for corporations, times the amount of effectively connected income allocable to the foreign partner. The foreign partner's share of effectively connected income is adjusted by any normally separately stated amounts associated with effectively connected income. As an example, an allowance for cost depletion, and any amount of income gain or loss reductions are allocable to a US partner and would be used to determine the effectively connected income. The amount with-held is then treated as a credit against the foreign partner's tax at the end of the year and is considered a distribution from the partnership on the last day of the partnership year.

Non-Residents

The tax rate on income not effectively connected with a trade or business is 30 percent of the gross income with no allowance for deductions. Applying this tax on the gross income makes it quite oner-ous. This income consists of dividends, interest, rents, royalties, annu-ities and other fixed determinable annual or periodic income. Many countries have different rates for dividends and interest that are lower than the US statutory rate. Thus, it is beneficial at all times to look for any treaties that might exist or to use countries with lower rates to reduce the onerous rates. If an individual is in the US for 183 days or more during a year, any capital gain is taxed at 30 percent unless it is effectively connected with a trade or business. If the individual is not present for the required time, the gains on disposition of capital assets are not taxed. An alien can elect to have income from real property treated as effectively connected. This election allows individuals to take deductions for depreciation, interest and other expenses associ-ated with property. Luckily, effectively connected income for residents and non-residents are treated the same.

If an asset is produced within the US, and that asset is sold abroad, a portion of the sale price of the asset is considered effectively connected. If a non-resident resides in the United States for less than 90 days, and earns less than $3000.00 per year for services, and is employed by a non-resident alien, foreign partnership, foreign office of a US person or foreign corporation it is not considered engaged in a trade or business. Any reimbursements of advances for travel, etc., are included in income as long as the individual is not required to substantiate the expenses. Capital gains that are effectively connected with the US business are taxed without regard for the time of residence. An alien who is taxed in the US must determine their tax by applying the different rates to the different types of income. When calculating their trade or business income the alien is generally limited to one exemption and must itemise their deductions. If it is an individual, they use the rates for a single individual. An individual who is married must calculate their tax using the rates for married individuals filing separately. Non-resident aliens must itemise their deductions, and unless they are residents of Canada or Mexico, they are not allowed any exemptions.

Foreign corporations having effectively connected income are taxed using the same rate schedule as US corporations and are subject to the same penalty provisions as their US counterpart. If the foreign corporation has passive income, it is subject to the same 30 percent withholding rate. If the US citizen holds stock in the foreign corporation, the citizen is not taxed on the earnings until they are distributed. For a foreign partnership, Trust, or Estate they are taxed at the same rate as if it were a US entity. In the case of the Trust or Estate an exemption is not allowed. The US taxes income on a Trust or Estate and the same rules apply as to individuals. The Trust can reduce its income by making distributions to its beneficiaries. These are then taxed to the beneficiaries. This is similar to Canadian Law and British law. Trust Estates are only taxed on undistributed income.

Estates and Gift Taxes

The rules for non-residents are fairly similar to those for residents, although several important differences should be recognised.

In determining taxable gives, only gratuitous transfers of US property interests are included. The ability to split gifts allows them to take a marital deduction for gifts disallowed for non-residents. The unified credits are different and only transfers to US charities are allowed as a deduction. The gross Estate includes only US property interest and does not include cash or certificates of deposit. The unified credit is smaller for non-residents and the nature of charitable transfers is limited to US charities. The marital deduction is not allowed, nor is a deduction for foreign death taxes. The remaining allowable deductions must be allocated between US assets and foreign assets. No deductions will be allowed unless the foreign Estate provides the Internal Revenue Service with an accounting of all assets, liabilities, etc.

Special Anti Avoidance Measures

The Code has a tax for unreasonable earnings accumulated by a corporation formed or established strictly for the purpose of avoiding income tax by not distributing earnings to shareholders. Taxes levied in addition to other tax imposed by the Internal Revenue Code, if the corporation is a mere holding or investment company, there is evidence of the forbidden purpose. The number of shareholders is irrelevant. The Code grants the corporation the right to retain earnings for reasonable business needs or statutory amounts of up to $250,000.00. This is applicable to all corporations, but it is difficult to prove a tax avoidance motive exists for a large corporation. The allowable non-earnings for personal service corporations is $150,000.00. This accumulated earnings tax applies to a foreign corporation if any of its shareholders are subject to US income tax audit and their distributions. The tax is applied on accumulated income that is effectively connected with a US trade or business. The foreign corporation cannot avoid the cumulative earnings tax by imposing another corporation between itself and its shareholders. The corporation which is owned directly, indirectly, or constructively by more than 50 percent is considered subject to the provisions where more than 10 percent of the earnings consist of effectively connected income. Any distribution received by an upper tier corporation is considered to be a US source income if the income was US source at the lower level.

The Code imposes an alternative tax on income for individuals and corporations. This tax is essentially what is considered to be a minimum tax. An individual starts with taxable income and adjusts for differences in recognition on income under the alternative system. This new system or alternative system has different rates for depreciation and amortisation and certain other expenditures. These differing rates as well as adjustments to gains and losses produce a new net income figure. Other tax preferences are added to this adjusted income, these preferences relate to tax incentives enacted by Congress that are subsequently judged to be subject to abuse. These amounts are normally excluded or deducted in determining income under the regular tax system and are added to determine the alternative taxable income. This income is then reduced by exempt amounts and the balance is taxed at an initial rate of 26 percent. When the taxable income exceeds $175,000.00, a 28 percent rate is applied to the excess. The exemption is phased out when the alternative income exceeds specified amounts. Corporations are also subject to this minimum tax although there are some differences. The rate applied for corporations is a flat 20 percent. The amount of the exemption is lower for corporations. The exemption is phased out at a lower level. Finally, the adjustments for tax preferences and timing differences will come from the same areas but are computed differently in most cases.

Subpart F relates to controlled foreign corporation rules designed to prevent abuse by US corporations doing business outside the country. To understand the workings of this part, one must understand how income tax was avoided in the past. Foreign subsidiaries could avoid US tax and any foreign withholding tax by holding back the income of the subsidiary to the US parent. When the corporation was finally liquidated, the income would then be taxed at the more favourable capital gains rate. This resulted in a change in the nature and characteristic of the income. Under Subpart F, a special class of tainted income is created. The stated income is then taxed to the US shareholder as if it had been distributed. For a company to be considered the subsidiary, it must be a controlled foreign corporation. A controlled foreign corporation is a foreign corporation that has more than 50 percent of its voting stock or more than 50 percent of its outstanding stock owned by US shareholders for at least 30 days. The US shareholder is an individual who owns directly, indirectly or constructively at least 10 percent of the voting stock on any day in the tax year in which the corporation was controlled. Each shareholder must report their rateable share of the controlled foreign corporation as Subpart F income and increased investment in US. This income can be treated as a deemed dividend on the last day of the controlled for corporations year and reduction in bases of the Code for control foreign corporation's stock. The shareholder is then allowed to take a tax credit for their share of the foreign taxes paid.

The Code divides the deemed distribution into five categories being income from insurance of US risks, foreign based company income, boycott related income, income described from illegal payments and income from other countries where for political or other reasons different or all privileges are denied. The foreign-based company income is also divided into five categories, being dividends, interest royalties, annuities, rents, and gains from sale of property that do not produce income or gains from commodities and foreign exchange. If a controlled foreign corporation has an excess of passive assets, the US shareholder must include in his gross income their share of the profits. An excess of passive assets exists where the adjusted base of passive assets exceeds 25 percent of the bases of all assets.

Other Special Provisions

The 30 percent tax on income received by a foreign corporation with a US branch is assessed. This rule is designed to prevent foreign corporations from avoiding the tax and dividend by operating through a branch rather than a corporation. The tax is imposed on the dividend amounts. That is the equivalent amount defined as the effectively connected earnings and profits of the US branch. The determination of the earnings and profits is made without respect to dividend distributions made during the year. The amount is then reduced by the extent to which earnings are reinvested in US assets and the excess of the adjusted base of assets over liabilities at the end versus the previous year. The new provisions apply to all income reduced by the treaty between the corporation's own country and the US. The Code contains a provision that allows the US to override such a treaty if the corporation seeks protection under that treaty when it is not a genuine resident of the treaty country.

The special branch level of interest charge was also enacted. A US branch is taxed and interest deducted in excess of the interest actually paid by the branch. In other countries this is referred to as thin line capitalisation on interest. The US law reclassifies the interest deducted by the branch as US source income and taxes the excess amount provided that 30 percent of the interest is treated as being paid in the last day of the year if payable within the time prescribed for filing the corporate tax return. The law also limits any modification to this tax by treaty. The provision does not override the treaty except were treaty shopping is involved. Treaty shopping is not something that is specifically defined. One should refer to the laws where the US does not consider a company a genuine resident of the treaty country, and can assume that the laws for treaty shopping are similar in nature.

Another method of sheltering income from taxation in the US is by using a third corporation in another country to generate losses. By generating losses in a third company the losses or gains can be off-set in the US pair. The law prohibits resident corporations from using losses to offset US income unless the corporations can demonstrate under the regulations that the foreign income was not reduced by the losses.

In addition to these laws the Code requires upon demand the production of the records necessary to correctly determine tax liability. Another attempt in controlling the abuse and avoidance or evasion of tax was to have laws requiring the maintenance, reporting and keeping of records. The Code also contains filing requirements and penalties associated with the non-compliance. Any foreign corporation or non-resident alien individual engaging in trade or business in the US must file a return.

New legislation is constantly being implemented regarding for entities such as corporations Trust Estates and individuals. A new definition over a resident Trust or resident Estate is already in the books. The new definition makes the determination of the residency status of a Trust straightforward and leaves the determination of the Estates residency status uncertain. A Trust is a US resident if the court within the US exercises primary supervision over the administration of the Trust and one more US fiduciaries have authority over all or substantial decisions on the Trust. The Estate is a resident if it is not a foreign Estate. A foreign Estate is defined as the state whose foreign source income is not effectively connected with a trade or business. For Trusts, one can see if the Trust documents gives authority to the US courts for monitoring the operation of the Trust, in which case it can be considered an American Trust.

CHAPTER 5
BRITISH INTERNATIONAL TAXATION

There are major similarities in the taxation laws of the United Kingdom, United States, Canada and other Commonwealth nations. This is not surprising as the history of all these countries have their roots historically in the British colonial efforts and system. British Common Law is a basis for law in all these countries and is used as a reference for precedence purposes.

As of March 1993, Britain closed its doors to allowing corporations incorporated in the UK, but operating outside its borders, a special tax-free status. As a result, there is an influx of corporations that have moved to the Channel Islands and other offshore centres to avoid taxation. These moves are taking advantage of the tax treaty between the United Kingdom and Jersey where it states that if a company is managed and controlled from Jersey, it is considered a resident of Jersey and not a resident of the United Kingdom.

There are three main concepts that are of importance in United Kingdom tax law that have importance to foreigners and tax travellers. These concepts are Domicile, Residence and Ordinarily resident.

Domicile

The concept of Domicile differs from that of residence in that an individual can only have one Domicile at any one time. To change Domiciles, one has to become domiciled in another jurisdiction. A person must have a jurisdiction of Domicile. Residence differs in that a person can give up residence without taking on a new residence. A person can also have more than one residence. To be Domiciled in the United Kingdom one has to give up their previous Domicile and physically move their residence to the United Kingdom with the intention of living there indefinitely. There is a presumption that in absence of proof, the Domicile of origin is the Domicile for life unless there is positive evidence of a permanent change. If you choose a Domicile and then abandon it, your Domicile reverts to the Domicile of origin. The Domicile of origin is the Domicile at birth of the father (and in some cases the mother). A wife also acquires her husband's Domicile as long as she has permanently changed her Domicile as discussed earlier.

If the person has the intent to return to their original country of residence and they maintain foreign citizenship it will usually be enough for the Domicile to remain in the foreign country of origin and not in the United Kingdom. When dealing with Domicile concepts, it is very difficult to determine intent and actually prove it. Intent is subjective in nature and without a true admission of intent is very hard to justify. Thus in planning, one should keep in mind that a tax traveller's strongest ally is their stated intent based on solid research and advice of what is best for their situation.

The United Kingdom established certain objective standards for determination of Domicile. The consequences of domicile are that the person is subject to capital transfer tax especially regarding gifts and Estates. An individual who leaves the United Kingdom is now considered Domiciled there for at least three years following their departure. In many circumstances it is best to wait the three years before effecting any transfers of assets where at all possible. Moving from the United Kingdom to Jersey, Guernsey or the Isle of Man does not change the Domicile. Another rule is that where one is qualified as a resident and present in the United Kingdom for at least 17 of 20 years, they are regarded as Domiciled there forever.

Resident

To determine whether an individual is a resident of the United Kingdom in a particular year, certain tests are applied as follows:

1. The first test, which is similar in Canada, is called the Sojourner's Rule. This is where an individual is physically present in the United Kingdom for 183 days (1 day more than 1/2 a year) or more in the taxation year. This physical presence does not have to be continuous. Its consequences are that an individual is taxable as if they were resident in the United Kingdom for the entire year.
2. If an individual is present for three months in each year over a four-year period they are considered resident for the period. Normally the authorities would only tax such an individual as resident in the fifth year if the individual has no previous record of residence.

It should be noted that there was a third test that related to the existence of an abode for use by the taxpayer. This test has been disregarded except to the determination of a person's intention.

Ordinarily Resident

This term refers to a person's normal habitual place where they reside. In Britain, it is not significantly different than resident. It is only when a person comes from abroad and is temporary in nature that it might have an effect. The concept is not defined. The tax traveller must be aware that it can come into consideration when a person is considered non-resident yet remains ordinarily resident and capital gains tax applies.

Residence of Companies

Until 1988, the test was central control and management. Subsequently, they implemented a law to specify residency of a corporation when incorporated in Britain, regardless of central control and management. Canada implemented similar laws in 1965. The exceptions to the rule are those corporations in existence before 1988 that do not carry on business in the United Kingdom (and Treasury consent was obtained), or those not resident after (with Treasury consent). Companies incorporated outside the United Kingdom continue to have residence status determined by the central management and control guidelines (where its real business is carried on). It is important to understand that in all residence situations, it is the facts of the situation that will govern the final determination of residency status.

Non-Resident Companies and Trusts

For gains from Trusts, settled by a non-domiciled United Kingdom resident, will there normally be no tax arising? In accordance with laws enacted in 1992, if a settler is domiciled and either resident or ordinarily resident in the United Kingdom at anytime in the year (this could be one day, although unlikely) in which a taxable gain arises to the Trust (called a chargeable gain), then S.80 applies and results in taxation. This section attributes the gain to the beneficiaries of the Trust who are resident or ordinarily resident and domiciled in the United Kingdom. This relates only to a capital payment, which is not one, that is normal income in nature. Examples of this are transfers of assets by sale or other means, conferring of certain benefits, and benefits on loans. Capital losses are normally allowed to offset any gains arising. One should always ensure they review S.69, which deals with the residence of Trusts, which looks to the location of administration of the Trust and the Trustees. The general rule is that if Trustees and administration is carried on from outside the country, chargeable gains are not taxable by the United Kingdom.

If the settler is resident or ordinarily resident and domiciled in the United Kingdom at anytime during the period when the funds are settled, then all the Trustees are treated as resident. The reverse is also true - if the settler is non-resident as above then the Trustee is non-resident. For Trusts that cease to become resident, there is an exit charge taxed on the basis of cost and fair market value at the time of exit. There is also a tax on beneficiaries of non-resident Trusts who receive payments from such Trusts that are subject to United Kingdom tax.

Chargeable gains belonging to non-resident companies will potentially have their shareholders taxed on profits and gains whether they actually receive them or not. These rules are similar in philosophy to the American Subpart F rules and the Canadian foreign accrual property income rules. The rules tax a person on such gains whether received or not if they are resident or ordinarily resident and domiciled and they own 5% or more of the shares of the non-resident company. These rules generally apply to what is called a *close company*, which is one that can be controlled by five or less *participators*. If a company is a public company, traded on a registered stock exchange, it cannot be considered a close company. A company cannot be considered *close* if it is controlled by one or more companies that are not considered *close* themselves.

Transfers

As a result of the recent rules regarding residency of corporations, many of the grey areas regarding the movement of business activities or capital abroad have been cleaned up and result in taxation when moved. In the past most of these transactions required Treasury consent, which was subjective in nature, with various vague guidelines for enforcement. The United Kingdom has followed the United States and Canada in changing such laws to prevent the ease of transferring activities and assets to the protection of an offshore tax haven. These laws do not fully eliminate the requirement for Treasury consent, as there are certain transactions that do not fall within the corporate veil and its encompassing rules.

The first category where Treasury consent is required is where a resident company causes a non-resident corporation, which it has control of, to create or issue shares or debentures. This would include advances from parent to subsidiary but not security given to a bank or insurance company in the normal course of their business. The definitions of terms such as *normal course of business* and *advances* are very important to the interpretation and use of provisions and should be closely reviewed.

The second category excludes transactions enabling a person to become a director. It requires consent for the transfer of shares or debentures to any person resident or non-resident. This would cover the sale of a subsidiary; prevention of artificial transactions designed to move control of the subsidiary. Any transfers within a group of companies are also covered as well as any other arm's length sale of shares and debentures at fair market value. Consent is not required for the emigration of a United Kingdom resident company, although there is a deemed disposition of all assets at Fair Market Value at the time of emigration for all assets of the company. These rules also cover the situation where a treaty makes a United Kingdom resident company non-resident for taxation purposes. In this case, as before, all assets are deemed to have been sold at their Fair market value at the time that they became non-resident. Collections of such taxes owing are not dealt with here except to say that the penalties for non-compliance are heavy.

The Tax Act imposes a tax on a United Kingdom resident who has the power to enjoy income of a person outside the United Kingdom. The term person includes in its definition corporations and Trusts. Thus any income whether paid or not from a Trust or company abroad must be included in income. To bring this section in to play, there must be a transfer of assets. The term *power to enjoy* is very broad in nature. It includes:

1. Any income being available for the benefit of the individual;
2. receipt or accrual of income;
3. receipt or entitlement to receive benefits from such income previously stated;
4. income where the individual has the right to invoke the power to receive it; and
5. any situation where the individual has the ability to control the application of the income.

If the company is set up for a genuine commercial purpose for trading abroad, these rules are not normally invoked. One should be warned that if the structure is made overly complex it will be viewed as an attempt to avoid tax and not a necessary commercial structure and it will be taxed. These rules apply mainly to individuals and will not normally be applied to United Kingdom corporations.

Corporate tax is levied at a rate of 31 percent on corporate profits of resident companies and United Kingdom income for non-resident companies. There is also a tax on dividends (ACT) which is normally approximately 23 percent but can be reduced to 13.75 percent where a tax credit is permitted by treaty. Interest payments are also subject to this tax at a rate of 23 percent to individuals and 20 percent to corporations. Other credits are allowed for dividends paid by corporations subject to the normal corporate rate of 31 percent.

The Inland Revenue will try to establish that a company has management and control in the United Kingdom for earnings within the country. This would allow them to assess a larger tax on the profits. If this cannot be done, they would then try to establish that the company was carrying on business within the country. That is, a non-resident is liable for tax for profits earned within the United Kingdom through a branch or agency. The key element here would be whether or not a permanent establishment was instituted within the United Kingdom. In evaluating this concept, one would look for any potential tax treaty between the countries involved, as the definition of *permanent establishment* is a normal clause in all standard tax treaties that follow the UN guidelines.

Another consideration is whether the company has an agent within the country. Such an agent is a company or person that accepts orders or habitually makes contracts on behalf of the foreign principle. If these conditions apply, the profits are taxed. The exception is where the agent collects a commission not less than the normally acceptable commercial rate. Thus, the Inland Revenue is able to collect its taxes from the resident agent and is therefore not worried about the offshore or foreign company. There are other more specific laws and, if cautious and careful, one can avoid the taxation of all the profits except the amount related to a commission or mark-up locally.

In the circumstances where there is business being conducted between or through a local company and a foreign company, it is important to note that the revenue authorities will subject such transactions to close scrutiny. If the movement and pricing of goods are between commonly controlled companies, the revenue authorities can ignore the pricing established for transfer and assign their own figure based on practice. Transfer pricing is a major issue within all foreign relations and is addressed throughout Europe, North America and others in their Revenue Code. One should note that with proper care and professional guidance these rules could be circumvented within acceptable limits of the law. In Britain, *transfer pricing* provisions also extend to property transactions, grants and rights, interest, royalties and renting or use of business facilities.

They key difference between North American rules and those of the British is the fact that the British only look to common control. Control in most instances is greater than 50 percent of the voting shares. In the US, these rules are not restricted to merely control (as they are in Canada also). The British will adjust the overall price for the transactions concerned, whereas the US and Canada will look to the overall profit. The US specifically will try to apportion the profit among the various companies involved based on what they consider a reasonable allocation of profit.

Interest, rents and royalties paid by domestic corporations to foreign companies are subject to a 25 percent withholding tax. These payments are allowed as deductions from profits.

Foreign Subsidiaries

This legislation is similar to the US Subpart F and the Canadian Foreign Accrual Property Income rules. It assesses tax on the profits of a foreign sub if 10 percent or more of the company's profits are attributed to the domestic corporation. Under these conditions, profits are taxed whether they are distributed or not. The rules do not apply for an individual although if a company owns less than 50 percent and individual shareholders make up the difference to get control, the rules will apply. Thus the concept of a controlling group applies.

There are several exclusions where taxation does not occur:

1. Acceptable Distribution Policy:
When 50 percent of profits for a trading company and 90 percent for any other company must be distributed.
2. Lower Level of Tax:
If local tax paid is less than 3/4 of the normal United Kingdom tax applicable.
3. Public Offering:
If 35 percent of voting shares are offered to the public and owned by shareholders who are not connected.
4. Exempt Business:
If it does not appear to be merely a set-up to avoid United Kingdom tax, taxation will not apply. If the company has a real operation in the foreign country and they have adequate local staff and other conditions depending on the nature of their business. The exception is leasing, dealing in securities and the receipt of interest income, dividend income or royalties. There are other restrictions such as the business should

not be primarily with associates in trades that are always domestic UK corporations.

5. The Intention:

If the proper intention exists then taxation can be avoided even if the previous conditions do not apply. The main motive being that if the intention can be shown as not to reduce United Kingdom tax then the exemption will apply. If the reduction is minimal, there is a strong argument to avoid the tax. It is possible to avoid the tax by incorporating in a country where there is a treaty with the United Kingdom. And the trading occurred in the other country.

Inheritance Tax

This can be important to foreign individuals and corporations as there is a transfer of capital or the rights to capital and income that could result in taxation. This tax is a direct tax on transfers that occur on death. The United Kingdom assesses a general tax of 40 percent on such transfers. One should be aware that transfers before death can be assessed also. Normally transfers within seven years of death (which can be hard to predict) are subject to what is called a chargeable lifetime transfer, including transfers to a discretionary Trust. Transfers between husband and wife are exempt where both parties are resident in the United Kingdom (an opportunity for splitting of income and/or tax). Individuals not domiciled in the United Kingdom are only open to taxation on property or assets situated within the United Kingdom. A very important issue as, at times, the assets can't be moved but the individual can. Certain bank accounts are also exempt.

Concluding Remarks

It should be noted that there are many similarities between the taxation laws of the United Kingdom, United States, Canada and others. This should not be viewed as a chance situation; it is an indication of an element of mutual co-operation and is an indication of co-ordinated efforts in the future. It is therefore imperative that proper advice be obtained from qualified professionals who can look to future developments. The user should always be aware that laws are changing rapidly in this area as the global economy is developing at an equally swift pace. What is relatively low risk today could be high risk in a short time. The potential savings are great, yet one must be prepared to incur additional costs on a continual basis as the structure requires alteration.

CHAPTER 6
LAWS OF CANADA

Residence

In Canada, the corporation or individual resident in the country is taxable on world-wide income. Thus, Canadian law assesses tax based on residency, as opposed to the US where it is based on citizenship. Income earned by non-residents, whether corporations or individuals, is taxed only on the income earned in Canada. Canadian taxation authorities (still known as Revenue Canada, but as of 1st November 1999 formally the Canada Customs and Revenue Agency) have made major aggressive moves toward stopping the use of tax havens in the past 10 years. Tax reform in Canada has basically followed in line with that of most other countries, especially that of the US. Because of close ties with the US, there are many similarities in the tax laws and there is an element of co-operation between authorities as far as exchanging and setting new laws. For corporations, taxation of foreign income involves a 25 percent withholding tax on distributions to non-resident shareholders. Canadian tax law imposes rates of up to 50 percent on individuals and 46 percent on corporations. As a result of perceived abuses, the Canadian Tax Act has added a general anti-avoidance rule to its legislation. In addition, Canada is a major player in the international co-operation of programs aimed at combating international tax avoidance and evasion. Canada has over 80 double tax agreements in force.

Canadian taxpayers should not be discouraged, as there are still numerous avenues for international tax planning. As a result of such initiatives, the US has influenced the Canadian authorities to renegotiate the Canada-Netherlands treaty to prevent Canadian corporations extracting profits that flow through Dutch holding companies exempt from Dutch withholding tax. This of course does not prevent flow through when they are subject to Dutch withholding tax.

Tax reform has been initiated to extend compliance enforcement procedures respecting international companies. One rule established was to reassess inter-company pricing transactions. In order to encompass a broader range, the normal three-year period was extended to six years disallowance. Revenue Canada can go back six years on such transactions. Another initiative, which follows that of the United States and New Zealand, was to allow a court order requiring disclosure of foreign-based information or documents with the proceeding being allowed as a civil proceeding in civil court to enforce the act. This makes it easier and quicker to enforce. Another area of disclosure has been regarding the annual reporting of inter-company transactions. This requires that every corporation resident in Canada, or carrying on business in Canada, shall in respect of each non-resident person, with whom it was not dealing at arms-length at anytime in the year, file within six months from the end of the year an information return containing prescribed information regarding that transaction (form T1 06 E).

The conditions required for residency of a foreign individual are based on the facts of each situation and therefore are governed by common law. The concept looked at by the authorities and courts are whether that person has truly severed their ties with Canada. They look at information such as location of family, location of asset and other factors that might reflect the true intention of the taxpayer. The meaning or extended meaning of residence also uses what is called the *solar juror rule*, which looks at the aggregate number of days stayed in Canada being more than 183 days. The words sojourned means to stay temporarily without actually becoming resident. This can be contrasted with the rules regarding part-time residence where such people are caught under Section 114 of the Act. If an individual stays temporarily in Canada for 183 days or more, they will be deemed to be a resident of Canada for the entire year and taxable on their world-wide income for the entire year, unless there is a bilateral tax treaty that provided for another treatment. Revenue Canada has specifically identified the following for conditions to be looked at

1. permanence and purpose of stay abroad,
2. residential ties within Canada,
3. residential ties elsewhere, and
4. regularity and length of visits to Canada.

In order for an individual to become a non-resident of Canada, there must be a degree of permanence in their staying abroad. If the Canadian who is considered a resident is absent from Canada for less than two years, there is an automatic presumption that they have retained their residence status abroad unless they can establish that they have severed their ties. If it can be proven that the return to Canada was foreseen at the time of his departure, they will presume that the ties were not severed. If an individual is absent for two years or longer, they will be presumed to be a non-resident of Canada. This is provided that they satisfy other requirements for non-resident status such as their dwelling, spouse, dependants, personal property and social ties having all moved abroad. An individual leaving Canada but retaining a dwelling place for year-round occupancy for their occupation or employment, by maintaining it or leasing it to non-arms linked party, is retaining the potential for being considered not to have severed their ties from Canada.

Leasing a residence to an arms-length party with the right to terminate the lease will generally not be considered to have severed their ties. If a married individual leaves Canada to work and their dependants remain in Canada, the individual will generally be considered a resident of Canada during their absence. An exception to this may occur when the individual is legally separated and has permanently severed all other residential ties within Canada. The residential ties of a single person are frequently of a more tenuous nature and, in the majority of cases, if such a person leaves Canada for two years or more and established residence elsewhere, it is likely that they will be considered as a non-resident of Canada during the absence. Generally speaking, an individual who leaves Canada to become a non-resident must not retain any residential ties in the former personal property (furniture, clothing, automobile, bank accounts, credit cards, etc.). Other relevant ties include such items as provincial hospitalisation and medical insurance coverage, seasonal residence, professional or other memberships in Canada, family allowance payments.

The courts have ruled that everyone must be resident somewhere and it is possible for an individual to be resident in more than one place at the same time. Accordingly, if a person does not establish a permit residence elsewhere, there is a presumption that they have retained their residence in Canada. Establishing a permanent residence elsewhere does not by itself mean that the individual has become a non-resident, as other factors must be considered. Where a residence is established elsewhere reference must be made to any tax convention or agreement that Canada may have with the other country. Once residency is established this status will not be affected by return visits to Canada, whether they are business or personal. Where such visits are more than occasional, this with other factors can be used to conclude the individual is continuing a residence in

Canada. For further information on the characteristics that need to be evaluated, the recent Canadian case of *Lee* v. *MNR* [1990] gives a listing of approximately 34 conditions that were evaluated in determination of residence. These conditions are as follows:

> ...past or present habits of life; regularity and length of visits in the jurisdiction asserting residents; ties within the jurisdiction; ties elsewhere; permanence or otherwise of purposes of stay abroad; ownership of dwelling in Canada or rental of dwelling in Canada on long-term basis; marital status and residents of spouse and children and other dependants; membership within Canada, churches or synagogues or recreational or social clubs or unions; registration maintenance of automobiles boats and airplanes; holding credit cards and other commercial entities including store cards in car rental agent cards; local newspaper subscriptions; rental of Canadian safety deposit box; subscription for life or general insurance including health insurance to Canadian insurance Co.; mailing address in Canada; telephone listing in Canada; stationary including business car chewing a Canadian address; magazine and other periodicals center Canadian address; Canadian bank accounts; active securities accounts in Canada; Canadian driver's license; members in the Canadian pension plans; holding director ships of Canadian corporation; membership in Canadian partnerships; frequent visits to Canada for social business purposes; burial plot in Canada; will prepared in Canada; legal documentation indicating Canadian residents; filing Canadian

tax return; ownership of Canadian vacation property; active involvement in business in Canada; employment in Canada; maintenance or storage of personal belongingss in Canada; landed immigrant status in Canada; sever your non severance instead sealed ties with former country residents...

Trusts and Corporations

Canada taxes Trusts as individuals in a similar manner as the US. Residency of the Trust is indicated by the location of the Trustee or other representative. That is, if the Trustee resides in Canada, the Trust is considered to be resident in Canada. If there is more than one Trustee, there is uncertainty as to its residence. In such circumstan.ces, the authorities would normally look to see which Trustee manages the Trust. There is limited case law on the subject except to the extent that it looks to management in control of the Trust to determine residency.

To determine the residence of a corporation, central management and control are the important factors. If a corporation was incorporated before 26th April 1965, corporate residence was determined by looking to the place of central management and control. Under this concept the corporation could be incorporated in another country, but because of the nature of its management structure it would be resident in Canada. After April 1965, the Canadian Act changed the provisions to provide that if a corporation is incorporated after April 26, it is deemed to be resident in Canada. Another rule interposed was that if a corporation incorporated prior to this date, and subsequently became resident by reason of it having its central management and control within Canada, it is deemed to be resident in Canada from then on. Another method of becoming resident is for a company simply to have carried on business in Canada after 26th April 1965, even if its central mind and management remains outside of Canada. If this happens they will be considered a resident. Thus, it is very tricky and one must insure that by having a passive interest in a piece of property they are not making themselves into a resident corporation. It has been held in the past, that even operating through the facade of a corporation, can constitute carrying on business in Canada and thus being resident.

The use of the Canadian-formed corporation, establishment of ancillary clerical facilities in Canada and acquisition of materials from a Canadian operating unit, even though used for other reasons, can result in being considered resident. This definition of central management and control cannot be found in the Act, it is merely derived from analysis of case law. The Canadian courts tend to follow the UK practices in the application of this test. The test by the UK courts was established in 1906 where it was said "a company resides for purposes of income tax where its real business is carried on. And the real business is carried on where the central management and control actually exists". Factors that are looked at by the courts are the place of incorporation, residence of the Shareholders, country of main operation, residence of officers and directors, place where Shareholders meet, place were directors hold meetings and place where books are kept. Canadian practitioners had been inclined to rely less on the measure of control of a corporation and more on the directors themselves, until it was made clear, in a later court case, that the matter of control was paramount. This has its premise on the fact that local directors of a foreign corporation can be mere puppets of the companies officers and that central management and control needed to be determined by the real facts and not simply by the local laws and regulations of the formed corporation.

It is important to understand that Canadian tax authorities will revert to the theory of sham where finding of a corporate residence using the central management and control test is ineffectual. For example if a company uses an Offshore shipment company to import a product. To effectively tax profits of the offshore subsidiary, Revenue Canada has successfully argued that the subsidiary should be ignored as a sham and its profits taxed as part of the Canadian operation. Although Revenue Canada has succeeded in some cases using this argument, they have also failed in some civil cases and in criminal prosecution case. Canadian residents looking to operate abroad through foreign corporation must establish substance as well as effective management and control in the foreign corporation. If this is not done its income may be taxed in Canada as if it were in the hands of the Canadian corporation. This is particularly the case where the corporation is based in a low tax country or country with which Canada has no tax treaty. In 1985, the Canadian Government further narrowed the scope of residence for corporations by adding this section to its tax act, wherein a Canadian corporation or a corporation in general otherwise resident in Canada, but exempted from Canadian tax under a double tax agreement is, deemed to not be a resident of Canada.

The attack against such dual residence companies takes the following approach:

>...for the purposes of this Act, a corporation other than a prescribe corporation, shall be deemed to be not resident in Canada at anytime, by virtue of an agreement or convention between the government Canada and government of another country that has the force of law in Canada, it would at that time, if it had

income from a source outside Canada, not be subject to tax on the income under Part 1.

The purpose of the legislation was to prevent corporations, whose dual residents would result as being favourable for the country of incorporation, from avoiding Canadian tax in respect of dividends paid by Canadian subsidiaries. This opportunity arose under the new Canada-US tax treaty when an arrangement was allowed wherein a US parent could interpose a US-formed special purpose holding company to hold shares of the Canadian operating company. Steps would then be taken to render the American holding company resident in Canada pursuant to the rules for central management and control. Dividends paid by the Canadian operating subsidiary to the US holding company would be free from Canadian tax by reason of domestic companies. Dividends paid to the American holding company to the US parent would also be exempt from tax for respective dividends paid by the Canadian resident companies. Accordingly, dividends paid by the American holding company as a resident of the US for tax purposes would be exempt from Canadian tax. The effect of the new section was to render the US holding corporation a non-resident for purposes of Canadian domestic law and the Canadian tax will apply upon the dividend payment by the Canadian operating subsidiary.

Departure Tax

In Canadian tax law, measures were taken to insure that emigrating individuals would not escape Canadian tax on all unrealised gains at the date of their departure. Canada imposes tax on many types of Canadian source income flowing to non-residents. Most income of an investment nature (interest, dividends, rentals) is subject to gross withholding tax. Individuals who were formerly resident in Canada are also subject to Canadian tax on amounts paid in respect of employment in Canada. This type of remuneration includes stock options and deferred compensation plans of all kinds. In Canadian tax the issue facing a parting individual is concerned with capital property. A person leaving Canada is deemed to have disposed of property at fair market value immediately prior to their departure. The reformed laws brought about in 1994 expanded the deemed dispositions to non-capital property as well.

There are some exceptions to this disposition. The provisions exclude what is called taxable Canadian property. Such property is subject to Canadian tax even if they never resided in Canada. Also excluded from the deemed procedure are individuals resident in Canada 60 months or less in the ten-year period immediately preceding their departure from Canada. This exclusion permits multinational corporations to assign personnel to Canadian operations for up to five years without triggering departure tax consequences. An individual can elect to postpone the departure tax provided adequate security is left with Revenue Canada and taxpayers are prepared to accept the consequence that Canadian tax will apply to any appreciation and elected property which arises after departure.

A foreign corporation that departs from Canada, or any Canadian formed company that migrates through export or corporate continuance, will be subject to the full liability for tax that previously applied only to exporting corporations. Where a Canadian formed corporation migrates by export continuance, it no longer will be deemed incorporated in Canada. To the extent that mind and management is no longer exercised in Canada, such corporation will after migration will no longer be subject to Canadian tax on the basis of residency. An exporting corporation that retains mind and management in Canada is not subject to the deemed departure tax but is subject to tax under another section.

Income

Foreign Source Income

In Canada individuals are taxed on their world-wide income which includes all foreign source income whether that income is brought back into the country or not. Resident corporations are subject to tax on their world-wide income including the foreign income, except certain dividend income from affiliated corporations. Canada also taxes on attribution based on the foreign accrual property income rules, which is accumulated income in non-resident corporations or Trusts. Such payments under the foreign accrual property income rules are taxable when ownership of 10 percent or greater exists in the foreign operation. This taxation becomes due when the income arises, not when it is distributed, and is not dependent on the income being repatriation into Canada.

The US has a great deal of influence on Canadian provisions although there are differences between the true approaches to the assessment of taxation. A controlled foreign affiliate is not quite the counterpart of control foreign corporation and there are other differences. The Canadian rules also differ from those in the UK. Although specific rules differ, there are similarities in the intention of the authorities in Canada, the United States and the United Kingdom. Under Canadian law, a non-resident corporation or foreign affiliate is defined as one that is non-resident and the Canadian resident has 10 percent or greater interest in any class of its shares. Other proposals regarding the affiliate rules would attribute the share ownership of

certain related persons in determining whether a non-resident corporation is a foreign affiliate.

The foreign affiliate is controlled by the resident taxpayer or
by that taxpayer if owned by not more than four other persons resident in Canada, or a related group of which the taxpayer is a member. Controlled foreign affiliate status also applies to any Canadian
shareholder with respect to which a non-resident corporation is a foreign affiliate if such a corporation is controlled by another Canadian
resident, whether or not related or dealing through an anonymous link
with this said Canadian shareholder. The act has not defined what
control is, as a result of court decisions it is in most cases considered
to be more than 50 percent of the voting stock of the corporation. The
foreign affiliate's income is not taxed in Canada until it becomes available to its main taxpayer, other than foreign accrual property income
of the controlled foreign affiliate by way of remuneration, interest, dividends and other means.

Foreign accrual property income is mainly income of a non-
business nature, investment income including most capital gains and
certain service income considered to have been derived from Canada.
Most important to the tax planner, and unlike the US practice, such
income does not include inter-affiliate dividends, nor does it include
payments of interest, rent, royalties, etc., made by one foreign affiliate to another. The payments represent deductible expenses of the
payer in computing its earnings from active business carried on outside Canada. In 1994 amendments to the foreign affiliate system
were designed to expand the definition of foreign accrual property
income to include income from investment business, income from
trans-shipment operations into Canada, certain interest, rents or royalties, and additional elements of income earned by offshore captive
insurance companies. The definition of investment business is intended to be very wide and target offshore portfolio investment operations

with exceptions only arising where the offshore controlled foreign affiliate employs more than five persons full-time in the conduct of such a business.

Included in the foreign accrual property income rules are payments by the foreign affiliate for services where the payments would be deductible from Canadian business income of the taxpayer or related persons in the controlled foreign affiliate. Insurance of Canadian risks is specifically included in the definition of services for this purpose. Imports and export activities involving Canada constitute active business operations, but the income of the controlled foreign affiliate or resident individual for services performed by that individual is foreign accrual property income. Capital gains derived from a controlled foreign affiliate, the sale of shares of another corporation which has foreign affiliate status relating to the Canadian shareholders, are excluded from foreign accrual property income rules, provided that substantially all of the property of the affiliate disposed of is used in carrying on an active business. Similarly any gain derived from the sale of a 10 percent or greater interest in a partnership, engaged in the conduct of an active business, is excluded from such rules. Such shares or partnership interests are called excluded property.

Foreign Trusts

The foreign accrual property income rules apply to Canadian beneficiaries of non-resident *inter vivos* Trusts after 1959, and testamentary Trusts arising following the death of the individual after 1975, where such Trusts have received property from certain persons. Discretionary Trusts of this type with Canadian beneficiaries are deemed resident in Canada subject to tax, as well as Canadian source taxable income and foreign accrual property income. A non-discretionary Trust is deemed to be a non-resident corporation controlled by beneficiary whose Beneficial Interest in the Trust represents 10 percent or more of the fair market value of all beneficial interest in the Trust. This would require that the Canadian beneficiary include their share of profit from foreign accrual property in income. The conditions of this section only apply where property has been received by a non-resident Trust for a person who was resident in Canada for at least five years prior to the year in which the question of foreign accrual property income inclusion arises. Thus, it is very important to those persons who immigrate to Canada. A person who is taking up residence in Canada may establish and non-resident Trust and be exempt from the foreign accrual property income attribution rules for the first five years of Canadian residence. This can be a major tax planning benefit for those people immigrating to Canada. Therefore, the use of emigration and immigration Trusts can be very important as a tax-planning tool for individuals who are international travellers. Clearly these types of tax planning benefits should be made with professional advisers as they are complex and can be tremendously beneficial for all those concerned. It is important to note that such transitional relief would not apply in respect of an interest in a controlled foreign affiliate, although foreign corporations may be combined with a Trust and benefit from the five-year exclusion.

This exclusion, in combination with departure tax rules for people who terminate residence in Canada within five years of entry, is also an extremely important element in overall tax planning for immigrants taking up residence in Canada temporarily. Time proved especially attractive to Hong Kong individuals who, because of the change of status of Hong Kong from Crown Colony to administration by China, sought establishment of landed immigrant status in Canada. This is also important for those doctors and other professionals who come to Canada for a temporary stay, if less than five years, as they are eligible for the use of such emigration and immigration Trusts and other tax planning techniques.

Foreign Accrual Property Income

Such earnings must be included for the income year of its Canadian taxable shareholders in proportion to the shareholders' percentage ownership in the affiliate's share capital. If the foreign accrual property income of the foreign affiliate is $5000.00 or less for the year, the Canadian taxpayer's participating percentage is nil. One should recognise that if such income has already been subject to foreign tax, Canada acknowledges that there is potential double taxation and allows a prescribed deduction for income rather than a credit against Canadian tax. This amount is determined by formula.

Foreign Dividends

Dividends received from foreign operations are taxable. If the dividend is from a controlled foreign affiliate and has already been taxed, a deduction is allowed. If the dividends received had been subject to foreign direct tax, a credit is allowable against the Canadian tax otherwise payable, assuming a tax treaty existed. In general, corporations resident in Canada are exempt from Canadian tax and all dividends received from a foreign affiliate prior to 1976. Dividends received from companies that are not foreign affiliates continue to be included in the recipient's income for Canadian tax purposes. There are three categories of surpluses the dividends can be paid out as for foreign affiliates. These are exempt surpluses, taxable surpluses and pre-acquisition surpluses. Exempt surpluses are made up of earnings from an active business carried on by foreign affiliates from a permanent establishment situated in a country that has a tax treaty with Canada, and after-tax undistributed earnings of the foreign affiliate for taxation.

Before 1976, certain capital gains and dividends received from the exempt surpluses and other foreign affiliates and other specified earnings were not taxable. Taxable surpluses are made up of active business income not qualifying as exempt surpluses. They also include non-active business income and 75 percent of capital gains derived from the sale of property used in an active business carried out in non-prescribed countries (non-treaty) and those from the sale of property not used in carrying on an active business. Any surplus that does not follow within these two is automatically included in pre-acquisition surplus.

What is the significance of the surpluses? Any dividend received by a Canadian resident from its foreign affiliates exempt surplus is not subject to Canadian tax. Dividends received from foreign affiliates taxable surpluses are included in a Canadian corporation's income for tax purposes and certain specific deductions are allowed (if it has already been taxed under the foreign accrual property income provisions the appropriate deduction is allowed). The regulations also prescribe the order in which dividends are deemed to have been paid out of each category of surplus. The corporate taxpayer may elect to consider that dividend income received and that it has been paid out of the affiliate's taxable surplus, notwithstanding the fact that some exempt surplus does remain. Thus, there is a possibility that this ordering can be changed. If a taxable dividend has not been entirely offset by the various deductions fore foreign tax, a further deduction may be available. If the shares of the foreign affiliate were owned by the Canadian corporation prior to 1976, the remainder of the dividend may be conducted for the adjusted cost base of the shares. This can be continued until the cost-base reaches zero. The effect is to delay the payment of tax and to change the nature of the tax. The delay would be to the time at which the shares are actually disposed of. The nature would be changed from dividends to capital gains tax.

When a Canadian disposes of shares of a foreign affiliate by way of sale or redemption, the gain recognised equals the excess of the amount received over the adjusted cost base of the shares. This is normally taxed as a capital gain. Canadian corporations can reduce such tax by electing the portion of the proceeds of disposition be treated as a dividend. This is advantageous where there is an exempt surplus in the affiliate being disposed of or sufficient underlying foreign tax in respect of taxable surplus. In either case, the effect will be to render the relevant portion of the proceeds either exempt from or subject to reduce Canadian tax. Canadian tax may be deferred completely when a foreign affiliate is disposed of to the extent that shares are owned by an intermediary foreign affiliate or controlled foreign affiliate. If the shares qualify as excluded property, the gain is not included in foreign accrual Property Income and 1/4 is included in exempt surplus. An amount equal to the underlying surpluses in the affiliate disposed of can result in an automatic election (S.93) that effectively leads to additions to the exempt surplus account of the selling affiliate. If shares of a foreign affiliate are owned by an individual, no such procedure applies and the full amount of the gain would be recognised.

Offshore and Tax Haven Operations

With the intention of blocking certain initiatives to create ownership of less than 10 percent and to avoid the foreign accrual property income rules, the Revenue authorities of Canada enacted legislation which required recognition of income in respect of offshore investment funds, regardless of the level of shareholders involved. These new rules do not attribute the actual income earned by the offshore fund, and instead they require inclusion of income of notional amounts determined by applying the prescribed rate to the cost of the investment. This section applies where the Canadian has acquired an interest in an offshore corporation, Trust or other entity where such interest

> may reasonably be considered to derive its value, directly or indirectly, primarily from portfolio investments of that or any other non-resident entity in: shares of the capital stock of one or more corporations, indebtedness or annuities, interest in one or more corporations, Trusts, partnerships, organisations, funds or entities; commodities; Real Estate; Canadian or foreign resource properties; courtesy of a country other than Canada; rights or options to acquire or dispose of any of the foregoing; or any combination of the foregoing and the motive for the investment can reasonably be regarded as avoidance of tax, assessed in accordance with the following criteria: The nature of the organisation in operation of any non-resident entity and form of, and terms and conditions governing taxpayers interest in, or connected with, any non-resident entity, the extent to which any income, profits and gains that may reasonably be considered to be earned or accrued, whether directly or indirectly, for the benefit of any non-resident entity are subject to an income or profits tax that is significantly less than the Income Tax that would be applicable to such income, profits

and gains if they were earned directly by the taxpayer, and the extent to which the income, profits and gains of any non-resident entity for any fiscal period are distributed in that or the immediate following fiscal period.

As has been illustrated, Canadian authorities have implemented certain measures to prevent the use of offshore bases to avoid taxation. These bases provided the tax authorities the ammunition to attack the misuse of tax havens. The main criteria are the use of the residence hurdle as a method of assessment, the dedication of artificial or sham transactions, the foreign accrual property income rules, and inter-company pricing. Canadians should take heart that there are methods that are still available for the use of offshore entities. Canadian residents who are shareholders of foreign corporations operating a legitimate business based in the tax haven will not be taxed on corporation income until it is made available to them in the form of remuneration, dividends, etc.

There is no Canadian tax penalty resulting from an accumulation of profits by a foreign corporation, nor any Canadian legislation that requires a corporation to distribute these incomes. The profits may be invested, and provided the income for the investment is not foreign accrual property income, Canadian tax will also be avoided. It is also worthwhile noting that any payments out of an exempt surplus of foreign affiliates will be tax-free in Canada. Any transfer of goods between two countries, especially if one is a tax haven, is invariably subject to close scrutiny by Canadian tax authorities. Even if it survives the residency test and is not a sham, it is often difficult to avoid running afoul of inter-company pricing provisions. The Canadian inter-company pricing provisions are not applicable if, for example, the Channel Islands affiliate uses a conduit for goods being exported to Europe, or a Hong Kong conduit is used for the transfer of goods from China to the United States.

Canada's tax revisions do not prevent the operation of holding companies. Interest growth received by one foreign affiliate from another foreign affiliate carrying on an active business is not foreign accrual property income. Loan interest from an American foreign affiliate to an Irish foreign affiliate would not be currently taxed in Canada. On the basis of the exemption from US withholding tax, any interest paid to an Irish company is not subject to Canadian tax. Other constraints imposed by various laws might be fairly minimal in impact. Only interest income is derived by the foreign affiliate is excluded from the Canadian foreign accrual property rules but it can also qualify for tax-free repatriation back to Canada if it is from exempt surplus.

This can be done with royalties passing between affiliates as well. Dividends flowing between foreign affiliates of Canadian corporations do not constitute foreign accrual property income. Thus, a dividend paid out of the exempt surplus of an affiliate in a listed country to an affiliate in a tax Haven which is not listed retains its character as exempt surplus and can flow through to the Canadian corporation free of Canadian tax. This approach is well known by most tax planners.

The Canadian foreign affiliate system allows non-Canadian business profits to be earned through non-Canadian corporations. Profits would be subject to withholding tax only when distributed by such company to an ultimate foreign shareholder. Where a Canadian subsidiary has accumulated profits that exceeded Canadian operation requirements, the concept of non-distribution of profits can be used to avoid tax. Rather than distribute the profits and incur a 25 percent withholding tax, the foreign parent would choose to use such funds to finance operations in other countries through the formation of foreign subsidiaries. Canada may act as a suitable base for investment in another country.

Another key section of the Canadian Act would be the rules for examining interest paid by a Canadian corporation on loans made by arms-length parties where no more than 25 percent of the principal is required to be repaid in the first five years. In addition to this there are situations where income derived by a Trust in Canada may be flowed to foreign beneficiaries without any Canadian tax.

CHAPTER 7
OFFSHORE CYBERTAX

Introduction

The use of the Internet, or Cyberspace as it is sometimes referred to, is the fastest growing medium for business. The term electronic commerce refers to all types of business conducted on the Internet. Offshore Cybertax is the tax considerations for the taxation of Electronic Commerce that evolves from cross-border and international situations. Typical examples of commerce range from the exchange of information, to the provision of software, to its use for advertising and promotion. This has come about as a result of improvements in international communication lines and the globalisation of the Internet from its use in universities. The Internet has proved that it can handle every form of digital information including text, sound, graphics and even music videos and movies. It is estimated that the Internet currently reaches over 1 billion people around the world. This number is increasing exponentially on a daily basis. Footnoting is used in this chapter exclusively for ease of detailed references.

The Internet allows commercial business to reach millions of potential customers through one simple medium. The taxation authorities of Canada, the US and many other countries are re-examining their traditional tax laws to maintain the integrity of their taxation systems. The Internet could provide opportunities for tax avoidance and double taxation.[1] Taxation authorities must also ensure that any conclusions they reach or adjustments to the system do not serve to impede the further development of the Internet as it represents the single most dynamic medium ever developed for domestic and international commerce. Of grave concern is the sourcing of income and whether a form of *tax toll booth* needs to be set up for the use of the Internet.[2]

Not only is the Internet generating widespread use, it is also creating a new way of doing business. There are many new products and delivery mediums unique to the use of the Internet. It is a frightening thought to taxation authorities and others in the regulatory institutions that the Internet has caused an increasing reduction in the significance of national borders for distribution or sales of a product or services. The definition of a traditional term such as a *product* is changing. It is no longer relevant, or at least easy, to determine if a company is offering a product, the use of intangibles or providing services. If a company sets up an office in one country, has communication links to a Web site in another country, a warehouse for goods in yet another and a line of independent, multi-product suppliers[3] of access to the Internet covering the additional territories, it would be very difficult to visualise the traditional concepts of jurisdiction-based taxation. A framework will need to be developed to determine which jurisdiction or country has the right to tax a particular transaction. Information or products that are purely electronic will be difficult to identify when there is no physical product to be shipped. Governments and other regulatory bodies have had a difficult time enforcing compliance of their laws on these intangible products.[4]

Some International tax concepts that need to be dealt with are:

1. Characterisation of income;
2. Determination of jurisdiction for taxation;
3. The types and nature of products; and

4. Developing some consistency and co-operation on an international scale.

Revenue authorities are trying to foster major discussions to try and deal with the problem of electronic commerce on an international scale. The US has issued policy statements on the topic[5] and has come out with a discussion paper on the implications of global electronic commerce.[6] The OECD has also released a report on the issue, and contributions to the discussion have been made by the Australians. Revenue Canada organised committees to discuss the issues and is interacting on an international basis to input into the debate.[7] Local taxation authorities of various countries have taken the position that the form of the transaction should not change the manner in which it is taxed. Some countries believe that existing laws are enough to handle problems arising, while others believe a more positive approach needs to be taken.[8]

Governments around the world are looking to attract this new medium of business. Many are using special tax laws to attract the business. Such attractions range from general reduced tax laws, as in Ireland, tax incentives offered by Canadian provinces, to the special features of offshore tax havens.[9]

Plan of Analysis

The remainder of this chapter will focus on an analysis of the issues that are of main concern to the taxation authorities of various countries. Solutions will not be presented, as it will be shown that it will take a great deal of mutual co-operation and sharing of ideas to resolve the problems electronic commerce on the Internet present in terms of base of taxation, jurisdiction and regulating the system in a cost effective manner. The following analysis is a discussion of the characterisation of income that is resultant from products or services on the Internet. Each product has unique characteristics, with new approaches to earning money on the Internet arising on a regular basis. An understanding of these basic characteristics should help to illuminate possibilities for solution in the future. The characterisation of income will also give insight into the interaction of the Internet and the standard tax treaties.

There will then be an analysis of jurisdiction. Before a method of taxation can be developed, it is important to know where the earnings will be taxed. The section poses possible problems for the reader to understand why the jurisdiction is difficult to determine. Key considerations for tax treaty purposes are the considerations of what *carrying on business* means and it's consequences. The final consideration is that of what constitutes a permanent establishment. If one can establish that a company or person[10] is carrying on business or has a permanent establishment in a location, it might provide a solution to the difficulties of electronic commerce.

The next section looks to the various broad types of products that might be encountered on the Internet. This is not an exhaustive analysis but provides a link between the characterisation of income, jurisdiction and the product. Whereas the first two sections examine basic concepts, the section following provides a more concrete idea of the characteristics of the products that one might find. To find a solution, all three sections must be brought together to properly understand the unique problem each presents. Products discussed are general goods and services and intangibles, software issues, including the problem posed by shareware,[11] online information services and finally database access.

Afterwards is a brief analysis of actions taken or comments issued by the OECD, Revenue Canada, Australia and the US on the subject of electronic commerce. The section provides insight to the initial position of the various bodies on the problem of electronic commerce. It is expected there will be many more comments by these bodies and others on the problems and possible solutions. This is followed by a section of concluding remarks and comments on the problem of the taxation of electronic commerce. A solution has not been suggested. The problem is in an early stage of analysis and it is hoped that the solution can keep pace with the changes in the technology. Remarks are put forth on the problems that can be expected from enforcement of any laws and some thoughts on avenues for sheltering of income if the status quo is maintained. In the end, it is for each government to decide on the path that they will follow, although it is hoped that communication and co-operation will be the key to a viable solution. It is suggested here that solutions will not be able to keep pace with the growth of the problems related to the taxation of electronic commerce on an international scale.

Characterisation of Income

Characterisation of income is important as it provides some understanding of what potential treatments are available for the various types of products that might arise out of electronic commerce. Examples used are not from electronic commerce as the issue has not been resolved as to the nature or breadth of the various types of income. The issue is of an on-going nature since the electronic commerce is constantly growing and changing in its characteristics. Discussions are first centred on whether funds are generated as income or capital. Once it can be determined that a portion is income, it is a question of what type of income will it be characterised as, and how it would be treated on an international basis.

Income vs. Capital

The first consideration regarding the acquisition of property from the Internet is whether it is income or capital. Many of the transactions in electronic commerce might involve the release of the rights to software or any other type of Intellectual property. If the exclusive rights given up are limited only as to time, it is likely to be considered capital in nature. The point where a payment for a right moves from income to capital is subject to a great deal of uncertainty. What is certain is that the greater the interest in rights given up, the greater the likelihood that the disposition will be treated as capital. Subsection 248(1) of the Canadian Income Tax Act[12] includes in property a right of any kind. It appears that most intellectual property could be included as property, but is it capital property or eligible capital property? Eligible capital property is not subject to as great a write-off as most other property. Class 10 or 12 of Schedule II of the Regulations to the Act include all computer software as being depreciable property. Revenue Canada consider that an outright sale of computer software can only occur where there has been an absolute transfer of all rights in the software and an unrestricted right to sell or lease the software is transferred. The courts in the Canadian case *Consumers Software Inc.*[13] looked at the treatment of the proceeds of sale of the taxpayer's rights to a computer software program. The company was in the business of selling or licensing software products that it developed and agreed to sell the source code to a software program that had been its major source of business. The sale included all ancillary pieces such as source code, object code, licenses, add-on programs, etc. The principals each signed a non-competition agreement. The court held that the proceeds should be treated as an eligible capital amount and since it had been received rather than paid, it would have been an eligible capital expenditure.[14]

One can conclude that most ongoing dealings would be treated as income in nature. It is only when a company sells its total rights to a product that has produced income in the past that it can be considered capital.

Royalty and Rental Income

When Canada signed the 1992 OECD Model Tax Convention, they were signalling a change in their historical practice of imposing a withholding tax of 10 percent on royalties. Canada reserved on the model provisions that proposed the elimination of withholding tax on royalties.[15] The government did not accept the OECD position on generic software.[16] The Department of Finance, soon after signing the OECD Convention, gave notice that in negotiating bilateral treaties it would seek an elimination of withholding taxes on payments that relate to computer software, and arms-length payments for the use of, or right to use, patented information or information that related to scientific knowledge.[17]

Canada's position on royalties is different from many other countries. Both the OECD Model Tax Convention and the US Model Tax Convention provide that royalties are to be taxed in the country of receipt. Eleven of the 24 countries (including Canada) have reserved on Article XII(1) of the OECD Model Convention, which calls for royalties to be taxed in the state where the beneficial owner resides.

The protocol on the Model Convention extends the exemption from taxation in the country of source to non arms-length payments in respect of patents and information.[18] Article XII(6) of the treaty is amended to give the place of use of the property for which the royalty is paid less importance in determining the situs of a royalty payment.[19] Article XII(6)(b) goes further to give the place where the property is used priority over the residence of the payer and the location of a permanent establishment (PE) that incurs the expense.[20] The protocol amends the paragraph to require that royalties borne by a PE are deemed to arise in the jurisdiction in which the PE is located. If royalties are not attributed to a PE or a fixed base, they are deemed to arise in the jurisdiction in which the payer is resident. If the rules do not result in the royalty being attributed to Canada or the US, and they are for the use of intangible or tangible personal property, the royalty will be deemed to arise where the property is used.[21] These pronouncements are intended to avoid double taxation in the situation where royalty payments are made to a third country.[22]

In the US, computer software, although not explicitly protected by copyright law, is viewed as a literary work and is protected from unauthorised duplication under the copyright law. Payments for software may be considered payments for products, the use of intangibles or the provision of services and depending on the specific facts it may be subject to withholding tax as a royalty.[23]

Rental income may be derived by non-residents and foreign corporations from the lease of tangible personal property. Access fees paid to a server are potentially rental income for the use of the server, as they are payments for placing information on a host computer. Furthermore, they can be considered as a lease of tangible personal property. A payment by a US payer to a Canadian recipient for the rental of a computer outside the US would be sourced to the country where the property is located and would thus be treated by American authorities as foreign source income. No withholding tax would be levied on the payments by the authorities in either country. If it happens that there is no treaty, how do they determine whether to withhold tax? An additional complication is added where the foreign host places the information on several of its computers in several countries.

The US also has its Foreign Determinable Annual or Periodic (FDAP) Income rules that capture fixed or determinable annual or periodic gains, profits and income. With a broad interpretation of these rules, FDAP income could capture many electronic commerce payments. If FDAP income is interpreted narrowly, very little would be captured. For example, payments by a US company to a Canadian online provider for electronic access to a database might be held by the IRS to be FDAP income on the theory that the payments are determinable and annual. They would also have to address the sourcing and nature of such payments to determine if they are eligible for a reduction under the Canada-US Tax Convention.

There is no definite answer as to whether an income item from electronic commerce will be considered rental income or royalty income. It is a matter of fact and each situation could be different. There is also a problem on an international scale of the different treatments and classifications that will arise out of electronic commerce. Another unsolved problem to be added to the list.

Jurisdiction

Once it can be established that income has been earned, there is a question of *where* it was earned. As can be seen from the previous section, different jurisdictions might treat the earnings differently. It is almost inherent that the jurisdiction for declaration of the earnings needs to be established. Electronic commerce presents a major barrier to this determination, as its nature is not physical. A further question is at what point will there be earnings and how much is allocated to each point. This section cannot provide an answer to this question for electronic commerce - it merely provides a basis for evaluating the conditions that need be considered.

Income Origins

The characterisation of a transaction as sale of goods or intangible licensing or service has important implications to the sourcing of income. The sourcing of income, in turn, has important implications to the determination of whether a country has jurisdiction to tax income and possibly the availability of any foreign tax credits. The sourcing of income has not been well developed for many products that have been around for years. Does this mean they should be included in a general category for determination or should the laws recognise the unique characteristics of each product and base the sourcing rules on the individual facts? This could place an enormous burden on the system. An example would be the sourcing of income earned on a piece of software. This software would be licensed to a foreign subsidiary of an unrelated domestic company. The software would be installed on the foreign subsidiary's computer that is located in a different country than where the subsidiary is located.

Would the treatment be changed if the software were to be accessed by users throughout the world?[24] Would there be an added complication if the foreign country where the software was installed is an offshore haven? The place of use could be considered the location of the computer where the software is installed (i.e. the offshore haven) or where the user is based. The problem of tracking the location of the user arises. Not only will the revenue authorities have a problem, the consultant or inside tax director, who is trying to deal with a number of sourcing issues, will have difficulty reducing the risk by increasing the level of certainty. For proper planning, uncertainty should be reduced or eliminated. In this instance, there is no assurance that any particular position will prevail. In fact, in light of the tremendous growth and change, it can be contemplated that no position can be considered to prevail for any reasonable length of time.

Canadian residents for example, are taxable on their worldwide income from all sources with applicable provincial taxes applied based on their province of residence. If a company or business operates in several provinces, the income is allocated using a formula with a mix of wages and revenues. Corporations using electronic commerce can take advantage of these laws by minimising provincial taxes. They can source their income in a province of low taxes using the unique characteristics of electronic commerce to their advantage. The corporation must have a permanent establishment in the desired province. A permanent establishment is usually a fixed place to carry on business. There is a question of whether a computer constitutes a fixed place of business. To reduce the risk from uncertainty of treatment, a business might attach the conditions of an office around that computer to ensure it is classified appropriately. That is that they might add furniture, employees and other conditions that would indicate a permanent office existed. [25]

Carrying on Business

Each country, or jurisdiction within a country, will have specific rules and practices that determine the guidelines for establishing when an enterprise is carrying on a business in that location. This is an important concept, as it allows the country to apply domestic taxation to business income earned there. For residents doing business within a country, the determination of carrying on business is fairly straightforward. In Canada, the Act dictates these conditions that apply to non-residents as follows: [26]

> For the Purposes of this Act, where in a taxation year a person who is a non-resident person:
>
> (a) produces, grows, mines, creates, manufactures, fabricates, improves, packs, preserves or constructs, in whole or in part, anything in Canada whether or not the person exports that thing without selling it before exportation,
> (b) solicits orders or offers anything for sale in Canada through an agent or servant, whether the contract or transaction is to be completed inside or outside Canada or partly in and partly outside Canada, or
> (c) disposes of;
>> (i) Canadian resource property...
>> (ii) property (other than depreciable property) that is a timber resource property, or
>> (iii) property (other than capital property) that is real property situated in Canada, ..
>
> The person shall be deemed, in respect of the activity or disposition, to have been carrying on business in Canada in the year.

If any of these activities are carried on in Canada, the non-resident will be subject to Canadian tax on taxable income earned in Canada.[27] Physical goods do not present a problem, such is not the case for electronic commerce transactions. Defining whether an electronic commerce operation is carrying on business in a location will likely create problems for the government and the business.

Another issue that follows would be the classification of income between that coming from property and income from a business. Each will have a different tax treatment. The question is whether income flows from business or from property. Electronic commerce requires a server, which is leased from a service provider. An assertion that the income flows from the electronic transactions created by the capital equipment (i.e. the server, or computer or other capital equipment required).[28] Durnford in his study could not find conclusive evidence in the common law to distinguish between property income and business income, although he did mention that if an independent service provider could be considered an agent, it could be considered business income.[29]

Ormrod[30] in his works asks whether a computer can act and, as a result, be considered to carry on a business. The Internet can perform many functions such as accepting credit card numbers, authorising delivery, making deposits, generating statistics, generating reports, etc. Is this enough evidence to make the supposition that the Internet can do the functions of an employee and be considered an employee performing a function? This issue is now being universally decided.

To connect a business to a place one must look to a particular place and the location where the contract is made. The taxation of Internet transactions has often been compared to a mail order business outside of Canada. There is a presumption that contracts are completed through the acceptance of the contract in the foreign location.[31] The catalogue could be compared to the Internet advertisement that is considered merely an invitation to do business. The offer to do business comes through an offer of payment and is accepted by completion and delivery of the order at the foreign head office.

Electronic commerce makes it possible to have a direct offer that may constitute a binding contract when accepted by the customer. It is thus possible that the result in *Quebec Pharmaceutical Association* v. *T. Eaton Co. Ltd.*[32] would be different if the Internet had been involved. The situs of the contract was found to be in Toronto, but if the Internet had been used in a similar manner, it is likely that the situs would have been determined to be Quebec.

The case of *London Life* looked at other tests to be used in determining situs, the accumulation of which would determine where the contract was carried on.[33] Constantine Kyres also included the following in the test: "...the location of the operation, the place of delivery, place of payment, place of purchase, place of manufacture, the place of solicitation, location of inventory, location of bank, etc..."[34]

This analysis did not take into account the use of the Internet and as discussed previously, there is an indication that it would make a difference. One should keep in mind that the principle of neutrality would oppose any difference in treatment. For electronic commerce, it is easy to control these criteria to ensure the transaction emanates from wherever management chooses. The common law is unclear, Canada has expanded its right to tax non-residents through an anti-avoidance rule.[35]

The case of *Sudden Valley Inc.*[36] uses the concept of soliciting orders as a serious indicator, in light of the relationship of the parties. Ormrod suggests that the use of a Web page would not fall within the definition of solicitation, since the Internet site is a form of advertising. Through the structuring of the Internet business operations, a user can be enticed to a foreign site and avoid these rules. It is likely that taxation authorities will change the rules, in an effort to keep a handle on potential manipulation.[37] The burning question is whether the taxation authorities are able to keep up with the rapid changes in the nature and structure of electronic commerce.

Permanent Establishment

Most tax treaties follow or come close to the OECD Model Income Tax Convention. Of particular importance are the recommendations regarding the *permanent establishment* (PE). The 1992 OECD Model Tax Convention under article 5 defines a PE as a fixed place of business through which the business of an enterprise is wholly or partly carried on. [38] This provides the concept of a fixed place of business with a certain degree of permanence. The mere presence of an organisation does not give rise to a PE, although it might do so if business is conducted through an agent, broker, or general commission agent, other than an independent agent. The agent must be acting on behalf of the enterprise and habitually exercises an authority to conclude contracts on behalf of the enterprise. It is unlikely that the solicitation of orders via the Internet would give rise to a PE. Advertising is normally seen as an auxiliary activity, as is the making of shareware or other software products available over the Internet.[39]

The current OECD Model Tax Convention does not deal with a situation where, for example, *Aco* in country A contracts with *Bco* in country B to have *Bco* run *Aco's* database on *Bco's* computer. It is unclear whether *Aco* will have a PE in country B. Arguments can be put forth that *Bco* is only providing *Aco* with the use of facilities solely for the purpose of storage, display or delivery of goods. It does not appear likely that article 5 was intended to deal with a database. If the data is considered goods, it could be argued the database is not solely for storage etc. as it can be searched and manipulated. It could be considered a PE.[40]

In most instances the business is partly run in the country where the database is run (i.e. through the computer). The argument is difficult to defeat, although, philosophically, can one consider a computer a fixed place of business under traditional terms? Authorities must move with the times as the traditional definition did not contemplate the computer as playing such a dominant role in the conduct of business, domestically and internationally. The definition might not even have considered the computer as a potential player at the inception of its formulation. This question will be subject to interpretation by the tax authorities and courts of each country. It is likely that some will conclude that the computer is a fixed place of business while it is also likely that some will not consider it a PE.

One can envision the emergence of this and other philosophical arguments that could play a major role in tax treaties. It is only through tax treaties that differences in the philosophical outlook of countries be resolved for the treatment of international electronic commerce. Where there is no tax treaty, the domestic law of the country will be used. A potential double taxation situation, with no relief through a foreign tax credit, results. For example, in the US, in a situation where there is no tax treaty, the domestic law concept of *engaged in the conduct of a US trade or business,* under Subsection 871(b) and Section 882, is used. A foreign corporation will be taxed at the graduated US tax rate on its net income that is effectively connected with its US business.[41]

It is also possible that a company located in country A, that has no tax treaty with country B, engages a service provider in country B to place advertisements on the Internet and to process orders, etc. This company may be deemed to have a business in country B, even if the provider is an independent agent. Local common law might dictate that where the production of income is active, substantial and continuous, it is considered operating through a PE. It is unclear whether such an argument should be allowed. The same logic may apply in the reverse situation.[42]

The Canada-US Income Tax Convention defines a PE as a fixed place of business through which the business of a resident of a contracting state is wholly or partly carried on.[43] The definition covers a permanent representative (i.e. an agent) who can conclude agreements on a foreign enterprise's behalf. Paragraph 7 of Article V of the Canada-US Tax Convention provides that a resident of Canada is not deemed to have a PE in the US merely because it carries on business in the US through a broker or agent. This rule applies as long as they were acting in the ordinary course of their business. Certain situations are specifically excluded from this paragraph. The definition of a PE in the Canada-US Tax Convention is in accordance with the OECD Model Convention's definition of a PE.[44]

Consider, for example, the situation where a company offers an online database through a computer in another country. As an alternative the company could rent space from a third party in the other country. Do the two possible approaches result in different determination of a PE? Under the terminology of the Canada-US Tax Convention, an Internet site that simply advertises a company's goods is not a PE. The classification as a PE becomes unclear where the Internet site can perform other functions such as soliciting and finalising orders or accepting payments to name a few examples.

Revenue Canada has asserted its right to taxation where a PE exists. The innovative user of the Internet would set up a system of fragmentation whereby each site is restricted to a particular task and all the sites together represent the completion of the transaction. Each site by itself could not be considered to be a PE, as it is merely performing an ancillary function. If the fragments are properly separated, it could allow a company to avoid the establishment of a PE under any of Canada's treaties (the US would also be susceptible to this scheme). One should note that the OECD Model Tax Convention has a provision that a PE may be established if the business is carried on through electronic equipment.[45]

The allocation of taxable income for non-residents in Canada is determined under Subparagraph 115(1)(a)(ii). Income is computed as if the non-resident has no other income except from the business in Canada. Expenses are apportioned to the business carried on in Canada. This apportionment is only to the extent that such expenses are from the activity of the business in Canada. For the Internet, it is more difficult to allocate the expenses. There might not exist any human activity in Canada, yet a business may be allocating a portion of their joint costs incurred to the Canadian operation. Canadian tax treaties override the domestic rules in Canada and therefore circumvent these problems. The PE rules in Canadian Tax Treaties require that the business be carried on in Canada before it can be established that there is a PE.[46]

Regulation 105 of the Act is applied where services are to be rendered in Canada. Withholding tax is applied where an agent of the service provider renders the service in Canada. This implies that the service must be done within Canada, and an implication of a physical presence requirement of the service provider or its agent. With electronic commerce, the interpretation remains unclear, as there might not be a physical presence of a service provider or an agent in Canada. For a fully automated non-resident provider, it appears that withholding tax will not apply. To summarise, if no PE or fixed base can be attributed to Canada, service income would be classified as business income that is exempt under the Canada-US Tax Convention.

Types of Internet Products

This section provides a brief analysis of the types of products that could be used or marketed on the Internet as a part of electronic commerce. Each product should be considered in conjunction with the characterisations from section 2 and the jurisdictional concerns from section 3, as they could result in different requirements to solve the problem of the taxation of electronic commerce.

Goods, Services and Intangibles

Physical goods cannot be delivered as yet by the Internet, as delivery is restricted to information and intangibles (although one can speculate as to the future - perhaps an electronic transporter is possible). Issues of relevance to the taxing authorities of different countries are the delivery of such goods, the use of intangibles or the treatment of the provision of services. This information is relevant to the determination of source of income, application of withholding taxes, determination of taxable foreign income and any potential application of custom duties. Goods imported to a country are normally not subject to withholding taxes. They could be subject to customs duties while royalties will normally be treated in the reverse manner. Royalties are subject to withholding taxes in many instances, yet not subject to customs duties. The existence of a permanent establishment in a country has an influence on the tax treatment. Services may not be subject to any taxes in a country as long as they are performed outside that country.[47]

For a Canadian company, income from the sale of goods, provision of services or royalties are all taxed the same under the Act. Any domestic need to distinguish between their nature would be influenced by the refundable portion of Part I tax available to royalty income or the manufacturing and processing profits credit available to goods manufactured or processed. Persons (including corporations) not resident in Canada are liable to taxation on their Canadian source income under Subsection 2(3) of the Act.[48] The non-resident must carry on a business and not be protected by a tax treaty. The question arises whether electronic commerce is carrying on business as opposed to income from property. Durnford maintains that there is no single characterising feature to differentiate between income from property and income from business.[49] Distinguishing business and property income is extremely important for the classification of electronic commerce for taxation purposes, as their treatment in tax treaties are different.

Software

Many mass-marketed, shrink-wrapped software companies have argued that they are selling goods with the idea that software is similar to a book which a purchaser is purchasing for their own use, and they are prohibited under copyright law from making copies for use by, or sale to, others. Revenue Canada's position is that a payment for software is not in substance a sale, but that it is a payment for the use of a secret formula and is subject to withholding tax under Subsection 212(1)(d).[50]

Relief from withholding tax can be obtained through the exemption in subparagraph 212(1)(d)(vi) which applies if the taxpayer also obtains the right to produce and reproduce the software. Revenue Canada's position has been questioned on legal and policy grounds.[51] In a letter in 1994, there is an indication that Revenue Canada has reversed its position regarding payments for the transfer of shrink–wrap software. They will accept such a transaction as a sale. Although Revenue Canada has reversed its position on shrink-wrap software it maintains its position that the use of custom software is subject to withholding tax.[52] Shrink-wrap software is generally packaged under a shrink-wrapped or plastic cover with a general licensing agreement included. Usually there is a notice that the opening of the document constitutes acceptance of the terms of the licensing agreement. The issue of why it is included as a sale is discussed in the protocol under article VII(1) of the Canada-US Tax Convention. By incorporating the exemption into article XII and focusing on its use, the Department of Finance is reaffirming its position that payments in respect of software are royalties, but that a treaty exemption may be negotiated.

The true characteristics of software are not clear in many cases. Different aspects such as the actual software, the license to use it or customised software are treated differently.[53] This has created a great deal of uncertainty as to how the transaction will be treated. Uncertainty is not what businesses like to have. The OECD, in its 1992 report on software, took the position that in most cases, payments for software should be treated as sales of products as long as the use of the software is personal. This position is expanded to include the situations where there are restrictions on the party's use. Payments for software that are to be further modified for commercial purposes are considered royalties.[54]

There can also be a discrepancy between the treatment by the source country and any other countries that are a party to the transaction. The courts in most countries continue to struggle with the treatment of software. Most software sales are made pursuant to a license agreement. The license agreement causes income generated as royalties. This can be varied by certain license agreements.[55] Where the service can be compared to a sale of a book, it would be considered as a sale of property.[56]   In the US, the Supreme Court ruled in *Wodehouse* and *Misbourne Pictures*[57] that payments for the use of copyrights resulted in royalty income, not income from the sale of property.   The court went further to say that if a transfer is for less than all the rights in a property of limited life, it was considered a royalty.   The IRS ruled in REV. RUL.64-56, 1964-1 CB (pt. 1) 133, that an unqualified transfer in perpetuity of an intangible can constitute a transfer of property under certain circumstances and in REV.RUL. 84-78, 1984-1 CB 173, that the right to an intangible must be in perpetuity to be treated as a sale of property.   Specifically, for software, LTR.RUL. 9231002 indicates that under certain circumstances, the license of software may more closely resemble a sale of property.

When referring to software, there are a number of components that are included ranging from the ownership of the actual software to the rights to its use. To add to the issues regarding the treatment of its component parts, there is a problem of determining the source of earnings on the transaction.   Software is easily transmitted through the Internet and does not require a physical component. International taxation of software transactions will continue to be a major problem for government regulators.

Shareware

The Internet has been a major cause of the popularity of shareware. It represents an industry of low technological programs that are offered through the Internet at a minimal or no cost.[58] Such software typically is distributed on the Internet with no controls attached. Shareware is usually promotional in nature and does not usually constitute a full workable system. It is either a promotional piece to show what the system can do if purchased or the basics of a system requiring updates to make it fully operational. The add-ons are what cost the user money. The classification of shareware becomes less clear for software as their value and use is limited and at times questionable. Any absolute determination is fact specific.

Online Information Services

Online information services range from huge multi-function commercial operators to simple bulletin boards or a simple provider of access to the Internet. The online service would probably be deemed a service as billings are generally invoiced monthly based on use. Either of the parties can easily terminate the arrangement, the service provider monitors and updates information contained therein, and there are few if any restrictions on the use of the information. The arguments against treating the payments as payments for a service are that the primary business of a provider is to grant their users a limited use of copyrighted material. The payment of the service provider to an information supplier can be a royalty or gain on sale of property. There is doubt in determining where the services are being provided and the true source of such income. [59]

Database Access

Several companies currently offer direct online access to databases for use by credit agencies, Lexis/Nexis and leisure products (i.e. games, music videos and magazines). Other products are also available with these services. The Internet is expanding its service from the domain of business to that of the individual consumer. Fees are charged to the consumer based on a variety of factors, including time spent on the CPU, the number of searches, files searched, etc. The

Wall Street Journal offers a service for access to their publication with a choice of various clipped features for the discriminating consumer and their particular preferences to information in the Journal. Other journals that can be accessed are mainly computer journals, although there has been a major influx of others since the Internet vastly expanded its market and capabilities.

It is very difficult to clearly classify payments for electronic database access as either royalty payments or services. Arguably, payments for an inquiry into a database of copyrighted material are payments for use of that material. Would that mean the payment is a royalty? Would the answer change if the producer provided the user with data and data-extracting and report writing tools? These would allow the user to access the information on their own. Therefore, the provision of tools is similar to the service provided by a consultant. Alternatively, the fee could be classified as the amount due on the sale of a product.[60]

The sale of a newspaper or magazine would normally be considered the sale of a good. If the magazine content is available on the Internet as electronic information, it can no longer be attached to a particular jurisdiction as it could be located on a system in the Cayman Islands. Access to the system would be based on the products a server has access to. There is also a problem of characterisation of the income. In the US, if the product is considered an intangible, the income would have as its source the place where the customer is located.[61]

International Pronouncements

The following is a brief review of papers and discussions conducted by the OECD, Revenue Canada, Australia and the US on the potential problems that electronic commerce presents. This is only the first step in what is expected to be an ongoing dialogue between countries in an effort to keep up with the changing nature of these problems.

The OECD Study[62]

The OECD report addresses what it sees as the top priorities for government action. These priorities will influence the taxation law regarding electronic commerce. The OECD report set out three priorities aimed at the regulatory environment of electronic commerce.

The first priority is to support opportunities for the growth of electronic commerce. They recommend that a government take a co-operative and practical approach to regulation to encourage actions that facilitate development and growth. Specifically, regulation of the information infrastructure, standardisation, information exchange, physical infrastructure and development of high-level action plans that reflect the pace of technical change in electronic commerce.

The next priority is the raising of the visibility of electronic commerce and promoting productive industry/government relations. Recommendations presented envision a partnership between government, industry and other participants in the private sector. The OECD wants to encourage the co-ordination of public and private sector electronic commerce activities. The opening of these communication lines would ensure flexibility in public/private sector relationships by promoting awareness, education and skills that will be necessary to reflect the influence of electronic commerce.

The final priority is to define new principles for the governance of economic activity in an electronic environment. The OECD sees governance as a major factor for maintaining marketplace efficiency and effectiveness. Issues addressed regarding this priority are the reforming of regulatory practices surrounding electronic commerce, clarification and revision of laws and regulations that affect the electronic environment, enforcement of laws within the medium of electronic commerce, protection of intellectual property and taxation.

The OECD supports taxation that focuses on the residency of companies and relates to the source and destination of tangible and intangible products. Their main concern is that the tax regime is workable and non-discriminatory. Tangible sales transactions and intangible sales transactions should receive consistent treatment that does not impact market environments. They are concerned with the use of tax havens as a result of the Internet, although the OECD has not been able to solve the problem. They are openly opposed to a bit or bite tax that would tax the process of data exchange. The use of a bit or bite tax is flawed in that the measurement is imperfect and can be easily avoided technically. There is also the problem of associating value to data for taxation purposes, which is difficult to determine what is taxable and what is not.

Revenue Canada's Advisory Committee

In a press release dated 10ᵗʰ April 1997, the Canadian Revenue Minister Jane Stewart announced the formation of an Advisory Committee on Electronic Commerce. The committee's membership includes individuals from a broad spectrum of Canadian business and government. The overall objective for the committee was to ensure the ability to collect taxes from domestic and international commerce. Their mandate is to:

1.   Review domestic and international trends in electronic commerce,
2.   Identify potential growth and use,
3.   Identify implications related to the risks on tax compliance,
4.   Examine the efforts of other countries, and
5.   Make recommendations that Revenue Canada should consider.[63]

The Minister of Revenue has stated that any proposed action should be consistent with the OECD, the Pacific Association of Tax Administrators, Australia and the US, and others willing to participate. Canada has participated with Australia and the US in making presentations to the OECD.

Australian Study

The Australian tax authorities started in 1995 to review the rapidly changing dynamics of electronic commerce on the Internet. The aim of the study was to address taxes administered, specific tax issues related to source of income, residency, permanent establishment, central management and control, evasion, money laundering, non-disclosure of income, the capacity of existing tax law to deal with such practices, and potential erosion of the tax base from commercial use of the Internet.[64] The Australian Commissioner of Taxation indicated that the study is responsive to an assessment of risks and pressures, including aggressive tax planning, electronic commerce, internationalisation of business and cash. The project focused on technological aspects of the Internet, financial aspects of its use and the legal application of taxation principles to the Internet.[65] The study examined the impact on compliance of Internet banking and finance systems and related issues including security, network bandwidth and auditability. Australia sought to examine challenges of electronic commerce on its tax system. They have considered issues related to changes to the legal framework in which taxes are administered. Their efforts have focused on the goal of ensuring tax principles are clear and the law is enforceable. Currently, they have directed their analysis on domestic concerns.

US Commentary

The US sees its multinational corporations as being leaders in the world. The corporations are therefore in the best position to exploit the benefits of the Internet through electronic commerce. The concern is that the American corporations will be attracted to many foreign Web sites. Canada would be one of their chief concerns because of the ease of commerce between the two countries. On 1st July 1997, President Clinton issued a Framework for Global Electronic Commerce (the Clinton Report).[66] The Clinton report made recommendations about various aspects of electronic commerce. In the field of taxation, the report recommended that the Internet should be a tariff-free environment when used to deliver products and services. It was felt that the promotion of a truly global medium through barrier-free trade would benefit everyone.

Since the US is a major player in this environment, one can surmise that they stand to benefit the most from such an environment. If this were not the case, would it be likely that they would change their philosophy? The report goes further to recommend that no new taxes should be imposed. Existing taxes that apply should be consistent across national and international jurisdictions. All domestic players should be involved in a co-operative effort to develop a uniform, simple approach to taxation based on existing principles.

In response to the Clinton Report, a press release was issued from the US Conference of Mayors (USCM). They contend that there is no evidence that existing local and state taxes impede the growth of the Internet.[67] The USCM were concerned that the President's belief that a non-regulatory, market oriented approach for the Internet should be carried down to the state and local level. Their view is highly politically motivated. The USCM's only concern was that the President, at the federal level, was dictating to the state and local level, thus pre-empting their local authority. The USCM did not approve of the President's proposals, as they felt it would cut a potential source of future revenue for states and cities. They have joined other state and local associations in a joint government-industry movement to set rules and regulations for electronic commerce. This could create problems of consistency among rules and regulations at all levels.

The basis for President Clinton's report was the Department of the Treasury Report of November 1996. The report was a comprehensive introduction to tax policy and administration issues resulting from electronic commerce. It was merely a forum for discussion of issues and the department encouraged comments and proposed solutions. The report focused on the following considerations:

1. Tax policy and administration and compliance issues taking into account technical and scientific characteristics of electronic commerce.
2. The neutrality of the tax system (i.e. similar income should be treated the same regardless of whether it is earned through Electronic Commerce or conventional channels of commerce).
3. Understanding that

> a) the Internet has no physical location or central control,
>
> b) a lack of intermediary institutions such as banks removes tax reporting obligations,
>
> c) registration requirements are easy to satisfy,
>
> d) Internet use can be untraceable and highly portable, and
>
> e) It is difficult to distinguish between taxable and other communication until the contents are converted from electronic form.

Administration issues addressed are the implications of electronic money, identity verification, record keeping, transaction verification and information reporting.[68]

Concluding Remarks and Comments

Enforcement

The US treasury has expressed concern that the Internet provides an opportunity for tax evasion. As a result, they are toying with the idea of a so-called tax toll booth on the Internet to ensure the administration of tax law. They would also like to restrict world-wide distribution of encryption technology by US programmers to reduce potential tax fraud. Today, the toll booths for Canada and the US are provided by customs. Duties are generally not imposed on services or the use of intangibles. Therefore transactions consummated electronically are not subject to duties. It is unclear why Electronic Toll Booths would be needed if such transactions are not currently taxed. If the Internet results in an explosion of potentially taxable payments by

Canadian individuals, the potential for lost revenue would increase. If this happens (which is likely), then there is a need for taxation authorities to adjust their tools to monitor the tax enforcement. Such adjustments must be made taking into account the concern relating to the impact of such measures on business in the Internet. An area for potential tax abuse is the advent of electronic cash. Since one cannot see or touch electronic cash, it is not be traceable by tax authorities. It is doubtful that the Internet will provide many new avenues for tax evasion, it is the lack of solid guidance on the treatment of electronic commerce that creates the potential for abuse.

Currently, the problem of rampant tax evasion has not reached epidemic proportions to warrant a change in the monitoring tools.

Sheltering Implications

In order to claim a deduction in computing income from a business or property, an expense must be made or incurred for the purpose of earning income.[69] A weakness in many tax shelters is that the acquisition price of the asset is excessively high. If there is to be a reasonable expectation of profit, the expenses cannot be so high as to render or create the expectation of profit unlikely, if not impossible. It is assumed that the onus is on the investor to show a reasonable expectation of profit. This will not be discussed here - it is assumed to be the case.

In the case where investors are putting funds together with the intention of making a profit, the first test to characterise the arrangement is whether or not a partnership exists and thus would the at risk rules apply. The definition of a partnership can vary by state pursuant to the appropriate partnership act. Usually built into the definition of a partnership is whether the co-owners carry on a business and whether it is carried on with a view to a profit. Revenue Canada, in a round table discussion, stated that the fact that the parties disclaim a partnership does not by itself mean that one does not exist.[70] Paragraph 3 of *Interpretation Bulletin* IT-90, dated 9th February 1973 stipulates that a characteristic of a partnership is a sharing of *profits* of a business, as opposed to sharing of *gross returns*.

At risk rules are based on the principle that losses will be deductible to the extent that a partner is liable. In terms of a limited partnership, this would mean that losses would only be deductible to the extent of the limited partners' at risk amount, in respect of the partnership at the end of a particular fiscal period for the partnership. An investor in a limited partnership is subject to the at risk rules where the limited partner owes an amount to the partnership or to a person with whom the partnership does not deal at arm's length. The limited partners are entitled to receive certain amounts for the purpose of reducing the impact of any loss the taxpayer may sustain by virtue of being a member of the partnership. In the case of most software tax shelters, the partnership has no employees and no ability to exploit the computer programs.

If a Canadian partnership intends to claim depreciation in respect of computer programs they will argue that the programs constitute software other than system software and is therefore included in Class 12 assets. The partnership will be entitled to claim depreciation at a rate of 100 percent. Since there is a half-year rule, as long as the acquisition cost is reasonable, the group can write off the costs over two years. If the exploitation of the software produces gross revenue that is royalty or leasing income, Regulation 1100(15) could limit the claim to income for the year from renting or leasing. Where a taxpayer has acquired something less than ownership, it is a question of fact whether the taxpayer has acquired a right to use or a right to market computer software.

If it is a right to market computer software, it will be included in Class 14 and treated as eligible capital property that has a significantly lesser write-off than Class 12. Revenue Canada expresses the view that a sale of computer software can only occur where there has been an absolute transfer of all intellectual property interests in the software and where the transferee obtains an unrestricted right to sell or lease the software. A sale does not occur where the transferor or any party other than the transferee maintains a proprietary right or there are any restrictions not normally associated with ownership (i.e. secrecy).[71] A licence to buy or sell, sublet or otherwise market software is not considered to be a right or licence to computer software.[72]

To avoid the leasing property rules, the software is not to be used and should not be deemed by any act to be used by the co-owners or partners principally for the purpose of gaining or producing revenue that is rent, royalty or leasing revenue. Software is usually considered akin to literary work with the same copyright protections, whether it is licensed or sold. [73]

If the partnership enters into an agreement with a US corporation to acquire an interest of up to 100 percent in the computer programs, and would be engaged to be the exclusive world-wide distributor and publisher of the programs, this arrangement is considered a joint arrangement between the partnership and the US corporation. It is unclear how the US authorities will treat the arrangement, although it appears that the partnership (as a party to the joint venture) and each of the partners will also be treated as carrying on a trade or a business in the US, with respect to activities relating to computer programs. The partnership's share of net income from the software agreement will be treated as income connected with the conduct of business in the US. The partnership will file US partnership tax returns indicating they are carrying on business in the US. Also to the extent that an individual partner is treated as having income that is effectively connected with the conduct of business in the US, that partner will also have to file the American tax returns as determined under US law.

In Canada, the sale of copies of the software is an activity that is conducted by each co-owner on an individual basis. If an arrangement is considered co-ownership as opposed to a partnership, each co-owner might be required to register with Revenue Canada for the GST, to claim input tax credits for GST paid on the acquisition of software. They will also be responsible for collecting GST amounts and remitting them.

Final Comments

Applications of current international income tax concepts to Electronic Commerce through Cyberspace are not easy. In view of the ambiguities regarding income streams, characterisations and sourcing of income to a jurisdiction, there are many interpretation problems that exist. For taxation authorities to properly monitor the streams of income they must first clarify the existing rules or develop new ones that will clarify the treatment and interpretation of the various products of electronic commerce.

Taxation authorities in Canada and Australia (to name a few) believe that fundamentally, the tax laws should not affect the structure of the market or commercial activities. The nature of the structure should not warrant different tax treatment. Taxation considerations should also not have an effect on the success or failure within a structure of a commercial venture. Although one likes to think that taxation does not affect these forces, it is a naive notion in its essence.[74]

Tax considerations tend to have a major impact on decision making and seem to have different treatment for different deliveries.

The best means have traditionally been the adoption and adaptation of existing principles instead of bringing in new or additional taxes.

It should be noted that the traditional approaches will most likely prevail in this instance. However, successful western economies are less localised, and the changing nature of business from one of domestic concern to concerns on an international scale is clear evidence that the conditions are changing on a larger scale and the traditional approaches will not work. The recent mergers of the larger US financial institutions and those of Canada are a clear indication of the trend.[75] The service industry is a prime candidate to electronic commerce use as they work with information, not physical goods.

Business will increasingly move from offices to electronic storefronts. PEs as currently defined, need to be reviewed and possibly adjusted to take into account the changing nature due to their non-physical presence by way of computers and Cyberspace. It is obvious that intangibles and intellectual property are and will be sold in new ways with new services included as part of the sale. Products provided from one country to another will be re-routed through another series of countries where a backlog occurs on the main line. Delivery of information is a major international consideration that could affect the tax treatment. If the information is routed through a tax haven, how will that affect the sourcing of income as well as the issue of tracking of income? There are no simple answers to how these problems will be solved as part of the answer depends on the evolution of Cyberspace business. The speed of Cyberspace business change would require the adjustment of tax treaties in many instances. It is questionable whether international tax treaties will be able to react in a timely manner to the growth in electronic commerce.

References on the Web

1. The Australian Taxation Office: www.ato.gov.au
2. Canada's Information Highway Advisory Council:
http://strategis.ic.gc.ca
3. Information Technology Association of America:
www.itaa.org
4. IRS Digital Daily: www.irs.ustreas.gov
5. OECD: www.oecd.org
6. Revenue Canada: www.ccra-adrc.gc.ca
7. US Treasury: www.ustreas.gov
8. White House: www.whitehouse.gov

CHAPTER 8
CHOOSING AN OFFSHORE:
CRITERIA ANALYSIS

As a summary of the complete discussion, it would be useful when choosing an offshore tax haven to put together a table for evaluating the choice. From reading the conditions set forth and discussed in the bulk of this book, it should be obvious that an actual ranking of offshore locations cannot be provided. It is the conditions, preferences and requirements of the user of the offshore that dictates the ranking. This chapter gives an overall illustration of how some of the criteria for choosing can be utilised to develop a ranking system. The details used are based on a particular client preference. The actual details of the client are not provided, as they are confidential.

Ahead in Appendix A is a detailed description of a computer program that was used to choose an offshore tax haven. This system was developed and used by the author for his clients. In addition, it gives the statistical analysis and relationships used to narrow the model down to 12 criteria for the situation analysed.

Analysis

In order to properly understand how this potential choice system works it would be beneficial to go through a semi-detailed analysis of 6 of the main criteria chosen by a survey of professionals in the field as being the most important in evaluation for an ultimate choice. Although this analysis deals with characteristics of offshore locations, it is important to understand the proper sequence of analysis to review the requirements of the client first before looking to those of the particular offshore countries in question.

One of the first characteristics to evaluate is that of communication lines. It is important for the tax traveller to understand what level of communication is required for the set-up they desire. For example, it is important to know the frequency of communication, the urgency of responses and response time, and the confidentiality factor in any communication. A person who is merely depositing money in a bank account and infrequently moving the money to another location or to a long-term investment vehicle does not have the demands of a business that is operating on a regular daily basis. Each has its own particular needs that would be dictated by the nature of the business, the product or service, the diversity of operation, the countries where business is conducted, etc.

Putting this all together in a tabular form with proper advance notice and evaluation of your needs will result in the best possible scenario with no major adverse surprises or blockages in the operation. One must realise that there are always unexpected problems, and with due diligence, these can be overcome. The first table (Table 1) and its accompanying totals are merely a simplistic view of what this approach would look like. Since it is difficult to determine the criteria of the reader, the tables will only deal with the evaluation of some offshore countries. These ratings will also change based on the particular preferences of the client. Preferences are such considerations as preferred location, preferred legal system, preferred climate, etc. It is usually best to consult a professional to help in determining needs as it is not easy to evaluate all your needs until it is too late. The use of an outside professional will reduce this risk.

For Communication you will note that the table has room for 6 criteria. In our analysis we have only used 4. It is estimated that the four main modes of communication are mail, fax, telegraph or telephone. Recently e-mail and the Internet have taking over as the most popular. In evaluating any characteristic it is essential to break it down into as many component parts as possible. This provides a greater degree of accuracy and reliability in the final result. For the analysis below, 200 professionals were consulted on their evaluation of the quality of the 4 communication criteria for the general characteristic of communication. Within this characteristic, each further breakdown is given a weighting factor as far as importance. The total of all weighting factors adds up to 100 for ease of evaluation. For example, in this case mail represents a weight of 15, fax 30, telephone 30 and other 25. To limit the possible range of choices for a rating, professionals were only required to break this down between Excellent, Good, Average and Poor, with a numerical value for each of:

Excellent	(E)	9
Good	(G)	7
Average	(A)	5
Poor	(P)	3

If more detailed information is available, these possible ratings can be increased resulting in a more accurate evaluation.

In evaluating the quality of mail service, considerations were made for speed of incoming delivery, outgoing delivery, chance of damage, possibility or risk of breakdown, strike potential for employees, likelihood of mail loss and available of other features (i.e. registered mail, special delivery, etc.). Considerations for fax are availability of fax, quality of transmission lines, the quality of line maintenance, quality of signal, breakdown possibility, etc. The telephone lines are susceptible to breakdown, and sometimes the lines are not so good so there is a lag in signal creating difficulties in hearing, as well as limitation on volume capabilities, security on the lines and concerns over condition of equipment. Finally, in the other category we would consider things like access to the Internet, existence of service providers and security on the lines. Note that the ratings given are based on a particular client preference taking into account their base of operation and other criteria. Ratings would change for each individual.

Table 1   Communication

Country	1	2	3	4	5	6	Total
Andorra	G	A	A	A			55
Bermuda	G	E	E	E			85
British Virgin Islands	A	A	A	G			60
Bahamas	G	E	E	E			85
Cayman Islands	E	G	E	E			84
Costa Rica	E	E	G	G			80
Guernsey	G	G	G	G			75
Hong Kong	E	E	E	E			90
Jersey	G	G	G	G			75
Liberia	A	A	A	A			50
Luxembourg	G	E	E	E			87
Liechtenstein	G	E	E	E			87
Monaco	A	A	A	A			50
Nauru	A	P	P	P			38
Netherlands	E	E	E	E			90
Netherlands Antilles	G	G	G	G			75
Panama	G	G	G	E			80
Switzerland	E	E	E	E			90
Turks & Caicos	G	A	A	G			55

Mode of transportation available for users is the next criteria of importance. This was broken down into 5 criteria being the frequency of daily flights, direct service to that location, travel time, number of carriers and dependability. Other criteria that could be added are the breakdown of these criteria by mode of transportation, including airplane, boat, train, roads, etc. This could expand the criteria to upwards of 20 criteria for evaluation. To use one of the island off-shores as an example, it is important to note that the modes of trans-portation are restricted to air and boat (in some instances hovercraft). Although there might be roads, etc., on the island, the criteria that has been used is for the traveller to arrive at that location from another place. Many offshore countries are not set up for visitation by trav-ellers, and for some this is not even recommended.

The weighting factors for these criteria were as follows:

Daily Flights	20
Direct Service	30
Travel Time	20
Number of Carriers	15
Dependability	15

Again, it is important to understand that these are the prefer-ences of a particular client. Many would consider that if it takes 3 or 4 hours to fly there, the difference is not important yet if it takes 6 hours and there is uncertainty whether the airplane will leave on time, it is of major concern. There are many countries and islands where the service is scheduled regularly, yet those who travel there frequent-ly will tell you that the airplane always leaves 2 to 3 hours late. In other instances, once you are on the island, leaving can be difficult as they always overbook the flight so even if you arrive on time for the flight there is no room. In cases, this author had to arrive 4 hours early to get on an airplane. Competition in airlines will usually reduce this risk, but not always. One should always be aware of the cultural habits and views regarding time as it can be very important in understanding the people. For example, in all fairness, the Commonwealth of Dominica and other Islands do not move at the same speed as North Americans and Europeans expect. If you try to push them, it will only result in frustration on your part, as things are just not done in the same manner or with perhaps the same expected dedication.

Table 2   Transportation

Country	1	2	3	4	5	6	Total
Andorra	P	P	P	P	P		
Bermuda	E	E	E	E	G		
British Virgin Islands	A	G	G	A	G		
Bahamas	E	E	G	E	G		
Cayman Islands	E	G	E	P	A		
Costa Rica	P	P	A	E	A		
Guernsey	G	G	A	A	G		
Hong Kong	E	G	G	E	E		
Jersey	E	G	G	G	G		
Liberia	A	A	P	G	A		
Luxembourg	E	E	E	E	E		
Liechtenstein	A	A	G	E	G		
Monaco	G	G	G	G	G		
Nauru	A	P	P	P	P		
Netherlands	E	E	G	E	E		
Netherlands Antilles	A	P	A	A	A		
Panama	G	G	G	E	G		
Switzerland	E	E	G	E	E		
Turks & Caicos	A	P	P	A	A		

The next criteria of importance is the political stability of the offshore. If there is a history of political instability or potential for change in the future, the question is whether a political change will result in major changes for the tax traveller and whether any new political party is likely to change the status, and perhaps seize all assets. It is normally not recommended by this author that assets be left in the offshore country for any length of time.

The criteria used for analysis are status of the current political party, likelihood of an insurrection, the degree to which the current state was a result of a popular election, the distribution of wealth within the country and the racial or religious harmony. There are many other criteria that could be inserted here, the intention is to add enough considerations to be able to have an idea of the political climate now and in the future. It would also be useful to have an idea of how far into the future this can expected to remain.

If the current political party is very popular and has been in power for many years, it is a good indication of stability. One can look to the differences in outlook of the opposition parties to determine the likelihood of changes that could affect the tax traveller. For example, in the Netherlands the difference in philosophy of the party in power and its opposition does not greatly differ in its beliefs regarding its tax laws. This reduces the risk, since if the opposition takes power sometime in the future, it is unlikely that there will be drastic change in the structure for offshores. It is also a plus if it was a popular election as it has the support of the majority. The distribution of wealth can be a factor as a nation with extreme poverty can be an added element to the risk factor.

Finally, one of the most important conditions is that of racial or religious harmony. Acceptance of wealthy North American investors is very important as resentment of their wealth or position provides stability and security of assets. Within the country there must be a strong element of racial and religious harmony as these are some of the major factors that increase the risk of using such countries. Many racial groups are resented in private especially when they are perceived as a group to be successful at the expense of others. Fiji is a good example of this, yet the USA, Canada, Britain and many European countries cannot be left off the list.

Table 3   Political Stability

Country	1	2	3	4	5	6	Total
Andorra	G	E	E	E	E		
Bermuda	E	P	E	A	A		
British Virgin Islands	E	G	E	A	E		
Bahamas	A	G	E	A	A		
Cayman Islands	E	E	E	A	G		
Costa Rica	G	E	E	A	E		
Guernsey	E	E	E	E	A		
Hong Kong	E	E	E	G	A		
Jersey	E	E	E	E	A		
Liberia	E	E	E	P	P		
Luxembourg	E	E	E	E	E		
Liechtenstein	E	E	E	E	E		
Monaco	A	E	E	E	E		
Nauru	P	E	E	E	P		
Netherlands	E	E	E	E	E		
Netherlands Antilles	P	G	E	P	P		
Panama	E	A	P	P	A		
Switzerland	E	E	E	E	E		
Turks & Caicos	A	E	E	A	G		

It was generally felt that, although it is difficult to measure, the attitude of the local people towards a major influx of foreign people and money is very important to the strength of an offshore location. It was found that if the locals resented the imposition of such wealth and intervention, it would not be a prime location to operate certain types of operations, especially those that required re-location of part of the operation locally. Attitude is a characteristic that would not normally have an effect in the short term, but it is one that will slowly fester and create problems in the 3 to 5 year period. In general, work done would lag and its accuracy would come into question, as there is no commitment or pride in the quality of work done locally.

Not surprisingly, the criteria we used for evaluation was:

1. financial benefit to the country   30
2. assimilation and acceptance into society   10
3. strength of tourist trade   30
4. commitment   20
5. ease of entry and exit   10

It is important that the local people are appreciative of the influx of finance and employment into their country as a result of these changes. They must also recognise the value and appreciate the change in standard of living. The influx of foreigners, with their higher standard of living and wealth, must be accepted by locals, without open resentment. It was found that where a strong tourist trade existed, there were much less problems. This was because the locals were used to the influx of foreigners and their money and the offshore trade was almost invisible to most locals. It is a proven fact that the strongest offshores have a good tourist trade, but of course there are exceptions.

Commitment of the people is also important to ensure that business can be carried on in an efficient and professional manner. Finally, it is always important that physical access to the offshore is not one riddled with administrative problems for entry and exit of people, money and goods from the country. At times, foreign companies might want to import labour and there cannot be major barriers to such moves. If local labour is the only option, it limits the flexibility and bargaining position of a company to get skilled and efficient labour when required.

Table 4   Attitude

Country	1	2	3	4	5	6	Total
Andorra	P	A	G	P	A		
Bermuda	G	A	E	E	A		
British Virgin Islands	G	G	G	E	E		
Bahamas	G	A	E	E	E		
Cayman Islands	E	A	E	E	G		
Costa Rica	E	A	A	G	E		
Guernsey	G	A	A	E	G		
Hong Kong	E	A	G	E	E		
Jersey	E	E	E	E	G		
Liberia	G	A	P	A	A		
Luxembourg	E	A	G	E	G		
Liechtenstein	E	P	E	E	A		
Monaco	E	G	E	A	G		
Nauru	G	A	P	A	P		
Netherlands	E	E	E	E	E		
Netherlands Antilles	E	G	E	G	G		
Panama	E	A	A	E	G		
Switzerland	E	G	E	E	E		
Turks & Caicos	A	G	G	G	A		

Business practice is an important consideration. Many countries are still at the level of third world countries for the elements required to conduct business. Since most users of offshore countries are sophisticated operators, they have higher expectations of the quality of operation. They can be very surprised, discouraged and at times consider ceasing operation there when confronted with different standards and the level of problems in business practices encountered. Typical is the speed of performing the simplest of tasks. Tasks that would be completed in a day in for example the USA could take 2 weeks in some of these locations. Backlogs from such slow operations can build up to over 6 weeks over the span of a year with an operating staff of double the normal complement.

Many business people have started to question the risk of collapse of operations due to their lack of confidence in volume and quality of output. Although these problems due exist, it must be accepted and not viewed as impacting upon the quality of work. Proper controls and an understanding of local attitude to business and work (and extreme patience) can result in a successful union of foreign and local complement. Other business factors are the quality of professional advice available locally and the number available. At times there are local guidelines for service fees that are high as a result of only locals being available.

For example, in one country all the lawyers charge a standard fee of 2% of the gross amount to register a property deal. For a deal worth 2 million dollars, this would result in a cost of $40,000.00 for a simple operation. At times, it might be beneficial for a group of offshores to bring in a lawyer themselves, who must satisfy local requirements and thus work exclusively at a lower rate. In addition to accountants and lawyers and other professionals, it is important that a good solid base of quality and honest office staff exist in that country and if operating within the country, other labour must also be available either internally and externally. The criteria used in this case included:

1. regular business hours maintained   20
2. quality of business & legal professionals   40
3. adherence to principles & quality labour   40

Table 5   Business Practice

Country	1	2	3	4	5	6	Total
Andorra	G	P	G				
Bermuda	E	E	G				
British Virgin Islands	E	E	G				
Bahamas	E	E	G				
Cayman Islands	E	E	G				
Costa Rica	G	E	E				
Guernsey	G	G	G				
Hong Kong	E	E	E				
Jersey	E	E	E				
Liberia	A	G	A				
Luxembourg	E	E	E				
Liechtenstein	E	E	G				
Monaco	G	E	G				
Nauru	E	E	E				
Netherlands	E	E	E				
Netherlands Antilles	E	A	G				
Panama	E	G	G				
Switzerland	E	E	E				
Turks & Caicos	A	G	A				

It is important to view the influence of other countries and any major industries on the operation of an offshore tax haven. A country that is dominated by one industry is susceptible to the politics within that industry. This can influence who and what type of operation can operate internally and externally with relative ease. Are the offshore people dealing with a government or do they have to be susceptible to the whims of a particular individual or corporation? In some south sea havens, permission has been obtained from the local chief to operate. Although operations are conducted by foreign operators and staff, who may be of a high level of competence and efficiency, they could be susceptible to the whims of a non-sophisticated person and his or her predecessor.

Other considerations adding to the risk factor are the influence of a major power on their operation and the internal operations of that major power to change things. For example, many of the Caribbean offshores are under the influence of British Rule. There are major movements by the US, Britain and others to encourage such major powers to exert influence on the offshores for better disclosure. The potential effectiveness of such measures can be difficult to assess. For example, even if an agreement for disclosure exists between governments, the local government might not require any disclosure by private professionals and their clients. This would nullify the effectiveness of the treaty. A good planner, through the use of several offshores, can avoid any current requirements and future changes. For offshore countries the future extends to a maximum of 10 years or less. The traveller should not be influenced by those persons claiming that the situation, as it is in the present, will last forever.

Basic criteria evaluated are as follows:

1. non-dependency on foreign financial powers   30
2. non-dependency on one foreign trade power   30
3. independent legislative system   20
4. independent financial sector   20

Table 6   Influence

Country	1	2	3	4	5	6	Total
Andorra	A	A	P	E			
Bermuda	G	A	E	E			
British Virgin Islands	A	A	E	E			
Bahamas	A	A	E	E			
Cayman Islands	A	A	E	E			
Costa Rica	G	G	G	G			
Guernsey	A	A	A	A			
Hong Kong	E	E	E	E			
Jersey	A	A	G	G			
Liberia	G	A	G	A			
Luxembourg	E	E	E	E			
Liechtenstein	E	E	E	E			
Monaco	E	E	E	E			
Nauru	G	A	E	E			
Netherlands	E	E	E	E			
Netherlands Antilles	A	G	G	A			
Panama	A	A	G	G			
Switzerland	E	E	E	E			
Turks & Caicos	A	A	E	E			

CHAPTER 9
THE REQUIREMENT AND USE
OF PROFESSIONALS

Offshore Wealth Accumulation and Security

Although this chapter gives details on the services an operation - such as that run by the author and his associates - can provide,
the embedded concepts provide the reader a stronger understanding
of what can be looked at and how offshores can be used. As an
example, this author and his colleagues provide financial and corporate services exclusively to sophisticated clients who want to avail
themselves of the vast selection of financial services available outside
of their home country. Our advisory staff are all qualified lawyer or
accountants, though due to the international nature and type of business, it is not a law firm. We, like other groups, are offshore specialists. A potential client may need our unique offshore financial business services for a variety of valid, legal reasons.

Needs for an offshore specialist team include:

- offered business strategies will make your business efficient
and retain more of what you earn
- early retirement
- independence from changing government policies (taxes,
pensions, regulations, exchange controls)
- security and strength of offshore financial institutions
- protection of assets
- confidentiality

- Estate planning
- favourable tax laws
- international business activities
- anonymity in ownership and management of assets;
- Trust law
- flexibility
- ease and security

Consultants make your offshore business interests as easy for you to deal with as your local business interests. A major offshore bank account is accessible as funds at the corner bank. The mystery is taken out through professional familiarity with foreign bank accounts, corporations, and legal systems. Clients enjoy a vast selection of financial services not normally available domestically. A client can be helped to put their money to its best uses and accumulate it at a much faster rate.

Consultants break the language and legal barriers of conducting business internationally. If the tax traveller requires a straightforward and relatively nearby services for a corporation, or something more specialised, such as a Swiss bank account or citizenship in a foreign country, consultants can make it happen.

No list is definitive regarding the services that can be provided. Each client is unique and the services attached are just as unique. A client's personal and business circumstances and mobility to design the best possible combination of services are all considered.

Some of the services consultants such as the author provide are:

- creation of vehicles that assure anonymity
- incorporation of offshore companies
- provision of foreign offices and foreign agents.

- maintenance of records and statutory filings
- nomination of proxy shareholder and director services
- offshore care of sensitive legal documents and papers
- captive insurance
- personal and corporate bank accounts
- personal corporate brokerage services
- international Trusts
- Eurobond and Euro currency accounts
- foreign credit cards such as MasterCard, Visa and American Express
- foreign cheque cashing
- foreign currency transactions
- offshore Trusts- letters of credit

Although this list is not exhaustive it represents the main services that most offshore operations require. Other vehicles can be developed depending on the particular circumstances and the creative approach to the development of such vehicles used. There are very few things or new vehicles that cannot be designed. Business is transacted for clients living in all the industrialised countries in the world. The most popular offshore jurisdictions include Aruba, Bahamas, Barbados, Belize, Bermuda, British Virgin Islands, Grenada, Netherlands Antilles, Turks & Caicos, and Vanuatu.

Consultants deal with an exclusive list of secure service-oriented banks and Trust companies in the world and will set up accounts for the management of your assets directly between yourself, financial institutions or fund managers. Devices will tailor an offshore plan for your special needs. The client is recommended countries with laws that are most advantageous. Bank accounts with a bank or Trust company felt to offer the best service for the client are established, and the client can always have direct control over their assets or have a stake in the care of dealings with the bank on their behalf.

Confidentiality

Sensitive legal information may be locked away offshore to protect the client's privacy. Information is kept confidential by advisers, who are legally bound by professional rules of conduct and duties of care (called fiduciary duties) to respect client confidentiality. Legal documentation is kept secure in the consultant's custody and control. The laws used offer clients unmatched security and privacy. At times foreign locations will be used to insure the protection of such documents.

Consultants are international in character. As an example, the author has offices in Canada, England and Grenada, as well as agents and associate offices in numerous countries around the world in order to properly service clients. Clients can be served by staff through the post, courier, facsimile, telephone, the Internet, or modem link, but these methods of communication are only used when the client has given specific authorisation to use them. They provide convenience of service so that the tax traveller may never have to leave their office.

The consultant should meet with clients on a person to person basis at least once. This of course is not necessary in certain circumstances as dictated by the client. For those clients that have specialised service and communication they may wish to meet more extensively on a personal basis and allow the consultant to make recommendations as to how things should be structured. For those who have a good idea as to how they want things to be structured, the consultant should be happy to follow their guidance.

Client confidentiality must be maintained at all times. Consultants do not reveal who their clients are nor where they are located or what business they are in. The utmost effort to insure the confidentiality and anonymity of all clients and their records is made. New clients can be given a general description of current and past clients so that they have an idea of the types of people that require such services. Most clients are honest people who have done well for themselves and many are usually innovative, have shown keen judgement, good business savvy, and have been very successful in whatever they have attempted. Such people require the highest of standards of personal service and consider confidentiality of utmost importance.

Types of clients that are serviced include:

- entrepreneurs
- industrialists
- families seeking ways to preserve assets
- families seeking to protect assets from legal and regulatory restrictions
- corporations and partnerships looking to do business offshore and abroad
- Estates
- people with accumulated assets through inheritance, lottery is or other business interests
- professionals on vacation
- professionals and others working offshore
- politicians seeking to set up live Trusts or to hold personal assets to comply with conflict of interest legislation
- fixed discretionary family charitable and personal Trusts
- non-profit organisations
- personnel working abroad

- any organisation for goods transported across international borders
- retirement planning

Integrity and Service

In order to provide integrity in international offshore services to clients, consultants should not provide domestic legal or accounting or investment advice, except in special circumstances. They should also avoid any strategic alliances that may jeopardise their ability and impartial knowledge in dealing with clients.

Clients have their own individual needs and unique circumstances. Consultants should not provide rigid pre-fabricated set-ups for clients. Each client should be assured that their situation is unique and that individualised service with careful assessment of their needs is provided. The satisfaction of each individual client should be the consultant's main goal.

Some of the main reasons for conducting offshore business and using the services of a professional offshore consultation team are:

- security
- protection of assets from political instability, legal harassment, public scrutiny and to maintain the rights of privacy
- confidentiality to maintain privacy and to preserve legal rights
- Estate planning to better care for beneficiaries, to freeze the value of an Estate

and to maximise the size of the Estate by minimising taxation, succession duties, and probate fees
- favourable tax laws to take advantage of laws where legally available
- offshore business activity in some cases facilitates the ease of doing business
- anonymity of ownership and management of assets can be maintained
- to take advantage of Trust laws that are more favourable
- to avoid changes in regulatory laws
- to avoid specialised tainting laws usually imposed by government regulation
- to provide a greater variety
- offshore banking services are not available locally

Approach to Planning

Offshore planning effects your most important resources: your financial assets. Clear lines must be established between the duties of the Trustee, or the investment manager or the adviser. There is a duty of care by all professionals involved to insure that instructions are carried out in a clear and concise manner. In exercising this goal consultants use an approach that minimises exposure to all types of outside parties, in order to obtain maximum confidentiality.

As previously stated, consultants must endeavour to maintain independence between all functions to insure against any apparent or actual lack of impartiality. It is imperative that the roles of financial manager and Trustee, where a Trust is concerned, should be separated. In this way there is no possibility of conflict of interest occurring.

By using the most advantageous Trust, corporation, and banking arrangement a versatile offshore vehicle is obtained. Conscientious consultants endeavour to insure that no one jurisdiction possesses sufficient information on the entire structure to pose a threat of disclosure. If one aspect of these elements is revealed, the remaining elements provide additional layers of screening and protection to insure that the affairs remain confidential and anonymous.

Potential clients can be reluctant to use such vehicles as they represent an unknown that they have no control over. With the professional capacity, expertise and desire for clarity, professionals can breakdown barriers and allow individuals and corporations to take full advantage of these lucrative opportunities.

Some Useful Comparisons

Banking

The client can open a foreign bank account that is convenient to use as their current local branch. Many people are under the misconception that they require a separate investment adviser in addition to their bank. Many offshore banks offer facilities for investment in shares, mutual funds and other vehicles that local banks cannot provide. Offshore banks can be contacted with relative ease by phone, fax or computer modem.

The use of foreign banks and international branches of major Canadian and US banks provide ease and expertise that cannot be found locally. The more sophisticated a bank, the less important its location. Access to banks can be through credit cards such as Visa, MasterCard, American Express, or other debit cards that can be used at machines world-wide. The consultant should not hold cash or assets personally but are merely a referral service between clients and reputable institutions where needed.

A Comparison between the Local Bank and Offshore Banking

Feature	Local	Offshore
Multi-currency management	NO	YES
Global investment	NO	YES
Full stockbroker service	NO	YES
Tax-free investment	NO	YES
Confidentiality	NO	YES
Safety from third party seizure	NO	YES
Credit card access	YES	YES
International teller machines	YES	YES
Asset protection	MAYBE	YES

The corporation in general has a distinct legal personality. It can be sued and it can sue. It has its own name, its own assets, and is limited in liability to the amount contributed by shareholders. It is, under the law, a separate entity. This separate entity protects the principles behind the company (the shareholders) and in most circumstances it transacts all forms of business without the personal intervention or personal guarantee of any individuals, shareholders or directors. The above is true of offshore and local corporations. The offshore corporation distinguishes itself by opening up international possibilities regarding trade, sophistication of institutions, reduction of exchange controls and other domestic barriers, the retention of confidentiality and protection of assets.

Contrary to popular belief, an offshore corporation is easy and inexpensive to maintain. The offshore corporation can take advantage of taxes in multiple jurisdictions by easily altering its form and structure to minimise taxes. As an added bonus, its business structures can be set up to preserve confidentiality through the use of bearer shares. Many offshore jurisdictions do not require shareholders, directors, or financial accounts to be filed with the government. The requirement of a registered office and shareholder register in most cases is also not required. These features allow maximum flexibility and confidentiality to properly operate an international corporation. Ideally, a single incorporator, director, or shareholder is allowed.

To summarise, offshore corporations allow the added advantage of facilitating international business, investments, loans, other financing, a purchase of goods, and general transactions with the maintenance of utmost confidentiality. Offshores also provide protection of assets through the use of bearer shares and nominee shareholders, limiting disclosure and creating a general corporate veil that cannot be pierced by outside individuals and government bodies.

Offshore corporations also provide facilities to hold assets internationally, in a favourable jurisdiction, including Real Estate ownership through the exchange of shares rather than exchange of assets.

This can be accomplished by parking title to the Real Estate in a separate legal entity, such as a corporation.

A Comparison Between Local and Offshore Corporations

Features	Local	Offshore
Limited liability	YES	YES
Freedom from Govt. intervention	NO	YES
Recognised internationally	MAYBE	YES
Shareholder confidentiality	NO	YES
Bearer shares	NO	YES
Tax-free status	NO	YES
Exempted from holding meetings	NO	YES
Bankruptcy protection	NO	YES
Creditor protection	NO	YES

Trusts

A Trust is a legal entity or arrangement where ownership is split between the Trustee and a beneficiary. The person establishing the Trust donates assets to the Trust to be managed by the Trustee. Instructions are given to the Trustee on how to manage and how to distribute Trust assets and income to the individual beneficiaries. A Trust has no share capital, although ultimate ownership of the assets lies with the beneficiary unless otherwise stated.

A Trust is normally used for administering family wealth for investment purposes, providing for the limited needs of a group of people, providing for various parties during their lifetime and beyond. A Trust is usually established through a written legal document that must adhere to the local laws where the Trust is established. If managed offshore, a Trust is governed by the local laws of that country. In Canada, the US and many European countries including England, there are restrictions on whether the original donator of property to the Trust can also be a beneficiary of the Trust. This is especially true when considering the tax laws. Canada and the US have experienced aggressive moves by taxation authorities to limit the use of local Trusts as a vehicle for avoiding taxes.

If properly created, an offshore Trust can transfer assets and investments to a vehicle that allows for the key relation of investment income virtually tax-free. This can also be done while maintaining compliance with income tax laws of the originator's home country (the originator is also referred to as the settlor or the original person who gave assets and set up the Trust). A Trust can also be used for the protection of assets and the exercise of Estate planning to freeze the increased value of a corporation in younger beneficiaries. A Trust can also be used to provide for family upon death (Estate planning).

In most cases, local Trusts do not protect assets from creditors or tax authorities and do not compound interest tax-free. Most Trusts also restrict transferring of assets, limit the life of the Trust, do not allow wishes and re-strict participation by the original donator or settlor in the management of the assets. Income on investments is normally taxed at the maximum rate of tax for individuals. Offshore Trusts do not have such restrictions. They normally provide protection from creditors, tax authorities, other third parties, and spouses where required. Investment income compounds tax-free. There is strict confidentiality, no limit to the length of time that the Trust can exist and maximum flexibility as far as management of the trust and ownership of the assets. Offshore trusts are usually used as an added feature of protection and maintenance of confidentiality.

General Recommendations

Many people who use offshore corporations or trusts restrict themselves to one vehicle or one individual country as a matter of cost-cutting. As a general precaution, this is not normally a good policy. It is usually best to set up several vehicles and at times several countries to be used with such vehicles to insure maximum confidentiality and anonymity. Many countries have excellent laws in certain areas but are weaker in other areas. For example, some regions make it inexpensive and easy to maintain corporations, but have weak banking systems and business ethics. Others are lacking in proper trust laws. For example, the author and his colleagues have recommended at times that clients use a trust from Hong Kong, a corporation in the British Virgin Islands, bank accounts in Switzerland and Grenada. At the time, this was the best vehicle for maintaining absolute security of operations. Due to changes in laws, this vehicle was altered to insure that the client was protected in relation to the current laws of all countries involved.

Examples of some of the scenarios that can take advantage of offshore locations are:

1.   An inventor or researcher who has developed a unique product or service that can be sold world-wide and is expected to produce large income;

2.   An oil worker who is located on a temporary basis at various oilfields throughout the world. Such a worker is normally under the impression that because the country they are located in to do the work does not charge income tax, they have no income tax obligations. In Canada, this is not true, as residency is the basis for taxation. If the workers do not give up residency, they remain taxable on income earned, in for example Saudi Arabia (that is, the Canadian taxation authorities can tax earnings in Saudi Arabia). If the worker is working for five months and returning to Canada, they normally would be taxable by Canadian authorities. Others, who relocate for several years are still potentially taxable unless certain conditions are set up. A worker who properly severs their ties with Canada should also be using an offshore location to protect existing assets from the country where they are located, and to protect future income when they return to their home country;

3.   A family with considerable assets located in various countries other than the country where they reside. The use of an offshore location provides added protection in the event of deaths, and insures easy transfer of assets with a minimum of tax, succession duties and probate fees.

220

4. A spouse in the midst of a lengthy and bitter divorce, finding him/herself in a position where most of his or her assets have been hidden, and he or she needs to protect the remaining assets from these and other parties;

5. A computer programmer developing a new program or game that is to be sold to a major manufacturer at a substantial profit that would be taxed substantially;

6. A writer recently completing a popular book and expecting to receive large royalties over the next few years;

7. Doctors and nurses going to Saudi Arabia or similar country for three to four years to work in those jurisdictions. Similar to No. 2 above, asset protection is required in the early years and protection of income from taxation could be required during their years of stay and possibly in future years when they return to Canada or another jurisdiction.

8. Surgeons, doctors and other professionals who are subject to liability regarding malpractice and negligence lawsuits can use offshore locations to protect a certain portion of their assets from potential liability;

9. Other people with substantial assets that need protection against impending inheritance tax legislation and probate fees;

10. Directors and other senior executives needing insurance and other protection of assets through a trust for a period longer than the normal limitation of life plus 21 years. Such protection will also accord protection of assets from potential director's liability that can arise from potential litigation circumstances

CHAPTER 10
WHAT EVERYONE SHOULD KNOW ABOUT TRUSTS

Offshore tax planning with Trusts offers many opportunities, but they do have pitfalls. There are mainly two broad categories of Trusts, those used for tax planning and those used for asset protection. These two are not necessarily separate as they do interact and therefore there are a variety of Trusts that are mixed in nature. Most countries would have three broad categories of Trusts for offshore, including immigration Trusts, emigration Trusts and inheritance Trusts.

Each of these would be subject to different local rules and have different benefits. They all shelter passive investment income and almost all are discretionary in nature. It is important that one ensure they have a very clear understanding of law of Trusts, the obligations, the duties imposed on the Trustee and the substantial exposure to claims of professional negligence. It is also very important to understand the local offshore Trust law. As a brief explanation, in most countries an immigration Trust is useful to shelter incoming capital gains for the first five years of new immigrants.

Typically, many countries have special rules for new immigrants whereby with appropriate planning they can derive a five-year tax holiday. Under these rules, new immigrants can establish an offshore discretionary Trust in an offshore haven and name their family as beneficiaries. The resident beneficiaries of a non-resident Trust do not have to pay any tax on the Trust's offshore income for up to five years. You'll note that this law depends on the country involved. It is important as well to determine what the term *new immigrants* mean in the laws of the home country. This would have major consequences as far as the Tax position of the taxpayer. For example, if one is earning 10 percent interest on your money and you had $1 million in savings, the tax on the earnings of $100,000.00 would be approximately $45,000.00. If the taxpayer could save this $45,000.00 tax for five years that would be in excess of about $200,000.00 in savings. To add to the savings, the earnings would be compounding, that is at the end of the first year that $1 million would now be worth $1,100,000.00, at the end of the second year it is worth $1,210,000.00 to the owners. After a five-year period this would be worth approximately $1,600,000.00. The rules regarding such Trusts are quite technical and one must be assured that the assets are not dissipated and/or misappropriated. The Trust requires the splitting of ownership of the Trust assets into its legal and beneficial interest.

An emigration Trusts works in the opposite manner. For a country such as Canada, a Trust is taxable on its income in Canada during the first 18 months after the Settlor (person who puts the assets in the Trust) of the Trust gives up Canadian residency. After the 18 months, the Trust is no longer subject to tax in Canada and income of the Trust accumulates tax-free in the offshore haven.

At this time the income and the capital of the Trust can then be paid to any Canadian beneficiaries on a tax-free basis. Using this vehicle to your advantage would involve setting up the Trust for a person's children who are resident of Canada. This is only Beneficial if you are leaving Canada. As such, if one has a substantial estate and is leaving Canada, it is beneficial to set up such a Trust in an offshore haven and name the Canadian children or others as beneficiaries. There are substantial reporting requirements on such offshore properties, and this would therefore generate work and fees for professionals involved to do compliance work.

The third type of offshore Trust, the inheritance Trust, is only for those fortunate to be left large sums of money by their relatives. The benefactor or soon-to-be deceased must be located offshore. The benefactor or establishing party set up a Trust in the offshore haven naming a Canadian as Beneficiary. The income of the Offshore Trust accumulates on a tax-free basis and any capital can be distributed to the Beneficiary without any liability.

As can be seen, offshore tax planning always involves complex issues of Trust law. Individuals can be attracted to set up bargain deals without realising what the potential problems are. Careful planning at the beginning can save taxpayers unnecessary financial and emotional hardships at a later date if the revenue authorities choose to attack the offshore arrangement.

Trusts are a very important vehicle in the use of offshore structures. As revenue authorities from the US, Canada, and the UK (as well as other countries) try to tighten the laws in an attempt to destroy the confidentiality and anonymity of offshore transactions, they will become even more important as an intermediary. To choose an offshore location for its favourable Trust laws it is important to understand the basics of what Trusts are all about. The following Chapter, although seemingly lengthy and complex, is merely a general overview of the complications of Trust law. Professional help should be secured.

Not all of the details need to be understood, and the Chapter merely gives the reader the option to understand how they work in detail or merely learn a very limited overview in order to evaluate the strength of the local Trust law in the location concerned. The basic Trust Law given, parallels the British System (although not exactly) as this is the base for most Trust law used in offshore countries. Once reviewed by the reader, it will be obvious that there is a need for professional advice in the proper design and use of Trusts.

Terminology and Basic Conditions

A Settlor is the owner of property. As an owner, a person has certain rights, including enjoyment, right to sell, mortgage property, and even to give it away as an "absolute gift". Some are with conditions that must be met. If you give a gift in Trust or to a Trust, it means you are called a Donor to the Trust.

The required conditions that must exist for the gift to be valid are:

1. The Donor must own the property, i.e. one can't give more than they own.
2. There must an intention to give up all the property you own (normally called transfer of property and delivery).
3. The intention must continue until delivery is made. Must be parallel to the operation of delivery. That is, must be able to show that right up to delivery of the property to the Trust, there was an intention to give it. This seems obvious in most circumstances, but there are many instances where this might not be true. The circumstances dictate.

If the Settlor/Donor doesn't give the property directly to the Donee, they give it to a Trustee to give to other persons called the Beneficiaries. The relationship between the Trustee and all other persons is a legal one (property, contract, torts).

The Beneficiary has no legal ownership in the property; ownership is vested in the Trustee. The Beneficiary has an equitable ownership and can enjoy the benefits of the property. The Trustee may not benefit from the property and the Trustee must protect and insure the property. Intention is crucial in a Trust relationship; the legal title becomes an equitable title given by the Settlor and split between the Trustee and the beneficiaries. The split of title consists of a 2-way transfer of title with the legal title going to the Trustee and the equitable title goes to the Beneficiary. To determine this, one should ask:

1. Was it the Settlors intention to Split the title or was it meant to be an Absolute Gift?
2. How is the Trustee responsible to ensure the Beneficiary enjoys the property?

Note that in an Absolute Gift the Trustee is not involved. In a split title, to be effective the Trustee owes a fiduciary obligation to the Beneficiary in the transfer from the Settlor to the ultimate Beneficiary.

Analytic Scheme of Trust Relations

The Trust relation is a fiduciary relationship that came out of the feudal system of land ownership. Trusts dealt with the use and enjoyment only and property was transferred for use only.

1. The Trust Relationship: The Settlor gives to the Trustee (who gets all legal ownership except an absolute gift- and has no right to enjoy the property) and then gives to the Beneficiary. The Trustee owes the Settlor a duty.
2. Fiduciary Duty: The Trustee has a duty of loyalty not to the Settlor but to the Beneficiary. The Trustee takes the property and must follow the terms as set out in the Trust document. The Equity courts supervise the duty of the Trustee to insure it is followed.

The terms of the Trust are the concern of the lawyers. Where a rule of Equity conflicts with a rule of common law, the rule of Equity prevails. For general reference, the common law is not as dictated by statute (legislation), it is the law that is determined through the use of court cases as precedents. Where actual legislation is established after the court cases, then the legislation overrides the common law. The reverse is also true, where common law is established after legislation, the common law overrides.

The relationship between Equity and Law (historically) are that Law acts on property; these are rights that are equal for all persons. Equity acts *in personam*, it acts on the conscience.

Equity

Equity is designed to:

1. Prevent fraud
2. Prevent mistake
3. Prevent breach of confidence (fiduciary)

Equity must identify a spatial relation, which is someone doing something contrary to conscience. Extended, Equity asks the question 'could the person have known?' If there is unjust enrichment (someone derives a benefit unjustly) and the Beneficiary gains by taking from a person, or deprives a person of something, or if that person promises to the Beneficiary and the Beneficiary gives consideration (money or property or something else of value), there are legal obligations. Equity enforces a duty of conscience (public). There is a duty of loyalty - a right to refuse property if the person intends to split the title.

The intent of the Settlor to trigger the duty of loyalty results in a Trust relationship. Trust in civil law is like a Cuckoo bird (that eats other birds); title can be split, that is the legal ownership can be split.

Kinds of Trusts

Making the best use of property and taking care of needs of Estates, i.e. grandchildren/ children:

1. Charitable Trusts: must have a public benefit
2. Trust Law: capital and income on property to beneficiaries by way of document or words
3. Statutory Trusts: those created by legislation.

Differences between Law and Equity

The Trustee has legal rights to use the funds but Equity will say that the Trustee took the property under the duty of loyalty and protection for the benefit of the Beneficiary. The court uses equitable remedies to enforce Equity. The main one is an injunction. There is no conscience with legal rights only in Equty (i.e. Breach of fiduciary duty). Equity holds the plaintiff not to pursue legal rights.

The Power of Equity can be through the inherent power of the court. A person can be charged with contempt (civil), and this is unique only to Equity. This would happen when there is a violation of an injunction. The main remedies of Equity are jail/injunction, specific performance, and equitable/subrogation. In law the only remedies are damages.

In the past, courts were combined and the judge had to wear two hats because there are two distinct systems

The Duty of Loyalty of the Trustee

The duty of loyalty includes the following considerations:

1. Initial Duties
2. Trustee Actions
3. Subsequent Trustee Duties

Standard of Care:

1. No delegation of duties
2. Invest
3. Impartiality
4. Account and inform
5. No conflict of duty

A failure to satisfy such duties equals a Breach of Trust.

As a general review of Trust law, the Settlor must:

1. own property (which is the object of the Trust)
2. the object can be a person or a purpose (i.e. a non-charitable Trust)
3. There must be terms of the Trust
4. Subject matter
5. Intention to establish a Trust must be certain by the Settlor (the intention must be to split the title)

6. The objects must be certain – described with certainty

The 3 certainties that must exist for a Trust are:

1. Intention to create Trust;
2. The subject matter must be capable of being ascertained; and
3. Those who benefit from Trust (called the objects) must be described with sufficient certainty

The Trustee has the responsibility of carrying out the duties which means the Trustee must have or be given powers.

1. An Express Trust: Must have some element of property. The person creating the Trust has expressed his or her intention to have property held by one or more persons for the benefit of another or others (Expressed orally, by will or by deed).
2. A Donor or Settlor can hold a Trust personally, or give it to a Trustee.
3. A Resulting Trust: The true owner; this is imposed by law (by operation of law) in certain situations when property results to the true owner.

There are 2 kinds of Resulting Trusts:

1. Those in which an Express Trust fails in whole or in part for any reason, i.e. Beneficial interest is not exhausted – to B in Trust for C for life – remainder reverts back to A (since the Trustee can no have the beneficial interest).

2.   Those in which a person makes a voluntary transfer of property to another or others or purchases property and directs that title be taken in the name of another or others.

It is important to consider that:

1. to return the property to the person who gave it and is entitled to it beneficially from someone else who has title to it.
2. *Inter vivos* transactions – no consideration = no intention to recovery of title – presumed resulting Trusts. When a person transfers property to, or purchases property but directs title to be taken in the name of, another and the latter pays no consideration, it must be presumed that the grantor or purchases did not intend to give the grantee the beneficial interest but rather retain it. The machinery to recover title is the "resulting Trust", i.e. husband *transfers* to wife - no longer an absolute gift - but the presumption of a resulting Trust – that must be rebutted, I.e. transfer to wife or child, or purchase made in the name of = a presumption of advancement rather than a presumption of resulting Trust. Gift is intended (no longer exist Re: matrimonial property law).

A Discretionary Trust is similar to an Express Trust except the Trustee is given discretionary powers (i.e. not specifically written and the Trustee has the right to exercise judgement). A Constructive Trust has nothing to do with intention but is imposed by law to prevent injustice. Most arise from a fiduciary relationship, i.e. Trustee and Beneficiary, solicitor and client, agent and principal, company director or officer and corporation, real estate broker and vendor or purchaser. This Trust may be imposed *to strip the fiduciary of any gains made* that belong to the Beneficiary (i.e. for misuse of confidential information – you are Trustee and you buy property that a Beneficiary was going to buy). Each case is dependent on the facts for a solution. In family law, one of the claims is that a Constructive Trust was created as a result of the circumstances of the situation.

Implied Trusts arise "by implication of a court of Equity", which are then further subdivided into resulting and constructive Trusts. This is not used. Statutory Trusts are for example one where all property, joint interests, etc., are used to pay debts and distributed to beneficiaries. Deemed Trusts deal with statutes. A statute may say that if truly a Trust, then certain consequences must follow or it may be a Trust without reference to a Trust. It is imposed by legislation to ensure that employers do not avoid various revenue and social obligations, i.e. amounts that employers are required to deduct for vacation pay and income tax are subject to such deemed Trusts. Deemed Trusts are necessary when at least one of the 3 certainties of a Trust is missing.

Trusts in the Higher Sense are only enforceable in the political arena, i.e. if the Crown is in a fiduciary relationship, the government may or may not enforce the Trust. The government can make it a "lower Trust", but must follow the 3 certainties. If a Statutory Trust is to be enforced, it must meet the Trust principles. To dispute this, one must prove the statute did not create a Trust.

The Legal Relationship of Power

1. Administrative power is the authority to deal with someone else's property (i.e. power of attorney – where the Beneficiary can do anything with the Settlor's property – usually under defined terms or mortgagee's power of sale).

2. Dispositive power is power over property - often used in a Trust (judges may use the term Trust power) - just be aware that there is a power relationship.

A is the Donor of the Power. B is the Donee or the recipient of the power. The Donor-Donee to each other is the power relationship. This includes

1. Power of appointment: Donor to Donee to appoint certain property. There are certain classes of persons who will be possible as appointees, including general, special or hybrid (remember that if the legal title is in the Settlor when transferred to the Trustee, it is split – legal title to the Trustee and equitable title to B).

2. Basic Scheme: in Donor- to Donee the legal title stays with the Donor who has power to appoint someone within the class. Then the legal title goes to the appointee. If it goes to someone outside of the class- the legal title stays where it is (Fraud – only requires a remedy for improper exercise of the power of appointment).

If the Donee were to die without exercising the legal title, power stays with the Donor. The Donor has 3 options:

1. Can make a general appointment to anyone, including his or herself. It is the equivalent to ownership – if you exercise that power. General power is like a gift (had to conceive of fraud on power).

2. Special appointment: test a person in a class or out of a class. Must go to someone of a particular class as long as person is in class and class is intelligible.

3. Hybrid: appointment to any person except an excluded class (the reverse of special, i.e. to anyone but those 3 cousins I hate)

Creation of an Express Trust

An Express Trust is one that is intentionally created by its maker (not a resulting or Constructive Trust created by operation of law). There are 4 requirements that must be met to create an Express Trust:

1. parties must have capacity
2. The 3 certainties must exist:
   a) there must be certainty of intention to create Trust
   b) there must be certainty of the subject matter
   c) there must be certainty of the objects.
3. The Trust must be constituted (the Trust property must be transferred to the Trustee)
4. All the requisite formalities must be met.

Requirements of the Creator of the Trust

There are three potential incapacities for the creator of a Trust: minority, mental incompetency and bankruptcy. Incompetency is the capacity to understand substantially the nature and effect of the transaction; one must have soundness of mind and understanding of the extent of the property disposing and comprehension and appreciation of the claims to which they ought to give effect. One must have the capacity to own property: a bankrupt can not be a Settlor and can not create a Trust to be used as a way to defraud creditors.

Any person capable of holding property for himself is capable of holding property as a Trustee, i.e. any capacitated individual or limited company can be a Trustee (unincorporated associations have no separate legal personality and are therefore incapable).

The Trustee must have the Power to distribute and appoint. The power of common law and power necessary in the Trust is specific to a Trust. At common law, the Trustee can not use property for illegal purposes. This special duty comes from the Duty of Loyalty.

The Beneficiary includes all persons, including minors, mentally incapacitated persons, bankrupts and corporations can be beneficiaries of a Trust - even unborn or non-ascertained persons. It can also be a purpose.

Considerations re agreeing to be a Trustee:

1. Capacity
2. Duties and consequences if you fail to manage properly
3. Must ensure you do not violate the Duty of Loyalty that includes no conflict of duty - the interest of the Trust must be central. The Court of Equity will enforce those duties.

Duties of the Trustees

The duties are onerous in nature and arise by virtue of the fact that Trustees have a duty of care. Trustees have title to and control over property belonging to another and must act solely in the best interest of that other person. This is the Duty of Loyalty and exists by law. The duties may be negated by a Settlor but this must be expressly (in writing) done. The Settlor has the right without intention to dilute the Duty of Loyalty. Equity is not there to say every Trust must be the same. The court will only fill in where the Trust terms are in doubt.

Some duties of the Trustee are:

1. obligation to perform personally
2. duty to invest the Trust assets
3. obligation to act impartially
4. the duty to account
5. duty to provide information
6. avoid placing themselves in situations of conflict of interest.

The Trustee must collect the assets for the Trust, ensure their safety, preserve and enhance their value. They must answer or do the following:

1. Review the terms of the Trust
2. Take an inventory to determine if it is all there?
3. Invest it in accordance with the provisions of the Trust instrument or statute.
4. Ensure property custody of the assets
5. Ensure there are no prior breaches of Trust.

Where there is more than one Trustee, they must act jointly; there are requirement for unanimous decisions - for every decision (to prevent deadlocks) if there is a deadlock they must go to court but must be careful: if a fixed Trust the terms are clear. If a discretionary Trust, Trustee will exercise discretion as long as they exercise proper standards. The Trustee can be removed and the court can appoint a new one. The courts are reluctant to interfere with the exercise of discretion by the Trustees and often they will only advise whether a power or duty must be exercised.

One should note that no Trust fails for want of a Trustee – only for intention of subject matter or object. The Trustee is an officer of the Equity court. If the failure of the Trustee to exercise the power would frustrate the intention of the Testator/Settlor or harm the interests of the beneficiaries, the courts will intervene.

Subsequent Trustee duties: A Trustee is not liable if they fail to exercise ordinary prudence with his own assets, but the Trustee is held to a standard of a prudent person. The Trustee is liable if ordinary prudence is not exercised. The Trustee is not held to a higher standard of care. There is no difference in standard even if they have knowledge or consult an expert. For example, if you buy a ticket from a travel agent, you expect a Trust relationship that the travel agent will buy your ticket on your behalf. The Trustee can not use a Trust account for his own benefit. A travel agent is not a Trustee to the airline if the airlines have not yet sent tickets. For a Bank, they cannot use money from your account to pay personal debts if the money in that account was actually for a specific purpose, i.e. money given to pay dividends. A person must inform the Bank if an account is a Trust account.

Co-mingling of funds means no Trust is created. If a Plaintiff gives a Defendant $40.00 and he put it in his wallet with his other money and the Plaintiff had said to hold it for Plaintiff's use, and then the wallet is stolen, the Plaintiff acquiesced when the Defendant put the money in with his own money. There was no Express intent to form a Trust. Intent means for a particular piece of property.

In a bailment situation when one gives property for a purpose, it is a contract relationship (like leaving the car at the garage). If the Bailee or Bailor dies, the contract ceases on the death of a party. If it's considered a Trust relationship, it continues. The key factor to determine whether or not a Trust exists are as follows: if there is no clear intention to create a Trust the court will find a bailment (no power of revocation in a bailment) - to make a Trust, there must be a clear intention plus duties, i.e. stocks and collect dividends).

If the Trustee sells property to a 3rd party, the bona fide purchaser has a better Equity title than the Beneficiary of the Trust. In a bailment, if one sells a car to someone else, the transferee can't get a better title than the owner because the Bailee doesn't have title.

An Executor takes title on the death of the testator and has full ownership to deal with the property and deal with the debts. The duty is on the executor to collect property of the deceased person to sell and raise money. The Trustee on the other hand, cannot sell Trust property to pay debts. If after a period of years, the executor's work is basically done, the executors become Trustees so that the items in question are not property of the Trust. If they sell the property, they do not have title to do so. The duties of an Executor lasts forever, never shirk liabilities and if a new debt arises, he has to pay new debt. He or she exercises the right to go to court and get property back to be able to pay the debts of the deceased. In an estate situation, a Trust has not occurred until the debts are paid, then the beneficiaries have an interest. Until that point there is no interest (creditors always have first rights).

Differences between an Executor and a Trustee: an Executor has no power to appoint another Executor unless they die. A Trustee can appoint a new Trustee and retire. The executor has full title (legal title absolute) - the Trustee only has split title and can't pledge anything.

Subsequent Trustee's Duties – Loyalty

1. standard of care
2. delegation of duties
3. investment
4. impartiality (Re: Beneficiary) capital and income decisions
5. accounts to inform
6. conflict of duties (no disadvantage to Beneficiary)

Standard of Care - Trustee must always put the best interest of the Trustee first (this is an objective standard) the standard of Care of a Trustee equals that of the ordinarily prudent person. If they seek advice from an expert, it does not raise the standard of care. If the Trustee is an expert, the standard of care in a professional area, they could be negligent.

Delegation of duties - no delegation unless sensible discretion in getting advice, must retain independence – A Trustee can reject advice. Trustee is liable if they delegate improperly. Must act responsibly and get advice where lacking knowledge and expertise.

Investment - should be prudent – show ordinary prudence – must have knowledge, skill, care, caution (risk aversive) in order to be protected from liability. The Trustee must take a risk aversive approach, that is, take all reasonable steps to protect the property before trying to make money. They can't go too far as they are dealing with the funds of another person and therefore must be more prudent.

Impartiality - fair and even handed between income/life tenants and capital holders. The Trustee is liable for restitution if proven to destroy the Trust.

Account and inform expense of Trust - statutes do provide compensation for breach of Trust. Both bear expense of keeping the

Trust. Duty to account - but no duty to give reasons. Trustee has discretion - only if the Beneficiary of the Trust alleged improper use, then reasons must be given in court. The Trustee must make decisions and argues on grounds there is no Breach of Trust.

Conflict of duty - Trustee can not put himself in a position of benefiting himself. Trustee can't deal with Trust property for his benefit. Must fully inform all parties. They should have independent legal advice. If minors are involved, they must appoint a guardian.

Trust and Powers

The powers outside a Trust: at law and Equity. The parties of Power given to a Trustee or to a non-person (power at law) are:

1. Donor of Power (owner of property)
2. Donee of Power (appointor of property)
3. Appointee (recipient of property)

In a Trust the parties are:

1. Settlor (owner of property)
2. Trustee (legal title/ onerous duty, discretion)
3. Beneficiary (equitable rights/ownership)

The Powers of Appointment:

The Donor of the power has the power to select who the Donee is (appointor of property) and the amount given. If the Donee dies, the power dies (as compared to a Trust that must continue indefinitely - no Trust fails for want of a Trust)

How to stop a power of appointment:

1. can cease on death
2. can release it any time
3. only get rights when appointed and this appointment when exercises properly, otherwise a fraud on the power makes it null and void.
4. must be made with a certainty of objects.

The Types of Power are:

1. power by person
2. power by Trustee
3. discretionary Trust

General Rules regarding Gift Overs (defined as a gift given upon an event happening):

1. If there is no Gift Over (can not logically deduce/imply there is one - because it must be clearly stated so that there is no doubt re; intent)- it is not automatically implied
2. If there is a Gift Over – there can not be a Trust power, only a mere power and a mere power fails if it is not exercised because nothing happens.
3. Look to the intention of the will, the words why the testatrix was selected, for example, some sisters and not others. It is used to help determine whether or not there is a Trust power or a mere power.

General Rule: If the Trustee has power to appoint and there is found to be a Gift Over, the Trustee then only has a mere power.

The test for determining whether a Testator or Testatrix intended to create a Trust or a power is:

1. Wording is not conclusive, but weightdepends on the facts
2. No Gift Over is also not conclusive Re: a Trust
3. Intention by language - and the court will imply only things necessary

In determining whether or not it is a power or a Trust- check these factors:

1. Language: what is the intention, specific or general (i.e. including certain sisters and not others), or could possibly exclude members of a class
2. If a Gift Over – there is a mere power – and no Trust.
3. If the Beneficiaries agree, they can collapse the Trust and take their shares or what they are entitled to (their property) - when they are *sui juris* and solely entitled to the property.
4. Discretionary Trust must distribute all property – discretion is in the power to select who gets what. Whereas a mere power, you don't have to give any power out.

Trustee with a mere power (power of appointment) still has duties to consider the facts in the circumstances (mere power is not as a Trustee of a discretionary Trust). Minimum duties:

1. obey the Trust instrument, understanding the terms
2. must consider periodically whether or not to exercise power

3. consider range of potential opportunity
4. if application comes forward, must consider that application.
5. check appropriateness of appointments.
6. how many objects must a fiduciary survey? Need a complete list in a discretionary Trust for certainty of objects. The test for power for persons is "In or Out Test" (or complete list or middle)
7. If the fiduciary fails to consider the exercise of power, then, the court will step in and first tell the Trustee to do it and if they don't the Equity court can replace the Trustee.
8. Court will look at outside party (3rd party) to look for an equitable solution.

Certainty of Subject matter: the intention will clearly identify the subject matter. When certainty of the subject matter is unclear, it can be cured by:

1. Constituting a Trust
2. Using the principle that Equity is equality

If you state that you want to leave 3/5 of net estate on death - we don't know what that is. The effect is a testamentary Trust - if an owner in property wants to establish *inter vivos* with the effect a testamentary Trust upon death, the Trust is invalid. All *inter vivos* Trusts are defeated if they take affect upon death. Assume it was a valid Trust: the subject matter will be void also because at the date Trust was made, the subject matter must be ascertainable. In an *inter vivos* Trust, you must have certainty of the subject matter when the property is transferred, and this must be transferred before death.

1. Deemed Trust: by way of statute the property is rarely identifiable. The government statutory authority over agents - government enforces the relationship by breach of fiduciary duty.
Equity will not enforce a deemed Trust but will only protect the
bone fide purchasers and creditors (government can not
supersede creditors unless they keep monies in a separate
account – and notify)
2. Uncertainty in the Quantum of the Beneficiaries' interest

Quantum: can be cured – but must be in Expressed terms - intention
clear and object clear, then there can be discretion in the subject matter.

Terms:

1. must find initial subject matter
2. look to the certainty of quantum. The Trustee needs to know
how much to give each Beneficiary.

Quantum is: what a reasonable remuneration for a Trustee would be.
Here, Equity won't allow Trustee to exercise discretion. The Testator
has two options - to make certain, the choices are:

1. discretion to Trustee must be given (as long as within reasonable limits)
2. give discretion to the court.

In order to establish the existence of an Express Trust, it has to
be shown that there had been a clear declaration of a Trust. Clear evidence of what was said or done to dispose of property must be obvious so that the Beneficiary would acquire the beneficial interest in it to

the exclusion of others, therefore the words "as much yours as mine" is sufficient to constitute a declaration of a Trust.

Express Trust declared orally:

1. Circumstances: unsophisticated - convey clearly a present declaration
2. Their relationship
3. Other factors of how property treated, i.e. shared jointly

Analysis:

1. If the man had owned it entirely for himself, it would all go to the wife
2. If he held it on Trust for himself and the "woman" half of it belonged to her, and not the wife.

Rule against a substituted Trust: if the intended transfer fails, the frustrated transferor is taken not to have intended to create a Trust for the putative transferee as second best. The Trust in lieu of a failed transfer "if he was sufficiently wide-awake to have thought about the possibility of a Trust in lieu of a failed legal transfer, he would be unlikely to have mishandled the legal transfer in the first place.

Certainty of Objects - One can describe a Trust that must be in favour of persons (not non-charitable purposes). There is a requirement that the class of beneficiaries be described in sufficiently certain terms that the Trust can be performed.

1. They must be clearly specified at the time of distribution, the Trustee cannot be sure that he or she is performing properly.

2. If the creator has not defined the class to be benefited in sufficiently clear terms, there can be no assurance that the intended class will get it.

3. The beneficiaries will be unable to join together and terminate the Trust once all are *sui juris* and absolutely entitled.

A Trust that fails to pass the certainty of objects test will fail and the property will result to the Settlor or testator's estate.

1. Fixed Trusts: The Class Ascertainability Test (a complete list) - it must be possible to ascertain each and every object (beneficiary) so that the Trustee can make a complete list of all beneficiaries. Trustees have no discretion. For a mere power to be valid one only needs one person to exercise power.

2. Discretionary Trust: Individual Ascertainability Test. There is now no need to be able to ascertain every member of the class of objects of a discretionary Trust. There is a similarity between the certainty of objects of a discretionary Trust to the certainty of objects test for a power of appointment. The individual ascertainability test may still fail if "the definition of beneficiaries is so hopelessly wide as not to form 'anything like a class' so that the Trust is administratively unworkable." Discretionary Trusts and powers of appointment held by Trustees are very similar in nature. (i.e. A Trustee need not distribute the subject matter of a discretionary Trust in equal shares).

The Test for certainty of objects - mere power of appointment among a class is valid if you can say with certainty that an individual is or is not a member of the class.   If it is a Gift Over it can not be a

Trust, it is equal to only a mere power. A mere power is not a Trust because there is no duty to appoint.

How does one determine whether there is a mere power or a Trust? Look to the intention of the will, therefore the Trust is for the benefits of the objects (beneficiaries). Once determined that it is a Trust the question must be asked, if it a gift to every member of the class (i.e. In a family situation – when you name all individuals – the general intention will be implied and divided equally). Did the Settlor intend to give equal shares or all objects to be equally considered?

Three things must do to find out who the beneficiaries are and count them and divide shares:

1. make appointments
2. consider appointments that come forward
3. check appropriateness of those identified

The court can step in and:

1. can appoint a new Trustee
2. can authorise representatives from a class to come forward for a scheme for distribution (beneficiaries to agree on something)
3. direct the Trustee to distribute.

The bottom line here is that the court does not decide who met the In or Out Test (this test merely asks the question who is included in the bequest as well as it asks who are the parties that are excluded) - they leave that to the Trustees to determine. The In or Out Rule says it is not enough simply to show someone is in but that you must also show who is out.

Whether a beneficiary can be included or they can not be included, you must be able to show they are not intended to be included. As long as there is a substantial number in, then it is OK. It doesn't mean a complete list is required, survey the range of objects.

Test: think of a Trustee doing his job, to make a survey, must have a complete list (to determine who is in or out - must have the list to make this determination)

Application - if you can't get a complete list, then there are problems with the in or out test.

1. A Trust does not fail simply because it is difficult to determine all the beneficiaries. Where there is a gift to a class, it must be possible to say with certainty whether any given individual is a member of the class, but it is only conceptual uncertainty and not evidential difficulties, which would cause a Trust to fail.
2. A Trust will fail when objects are conceptual uncertainty
3. A Trust will not fail if there is evidentiary uncertainty unless the Trust is hopelessly unworkable (i.e. residents of Greater London). That is, it is too capricious and too onerous a duty for the Trustee (too large - can't make sense of this). May be OK if the Trustee happens to be the Chairperson of the London Council and has special knowledge.

Sample Analysis:

1. $10,000.00 held in thrust for the members of family in equal shares. Given in Trust equals a split title in a fixed Trust. Step 1 - If it is a fixed Trust: the subject is in equal

shares/object is the beneficiary, there is no discretion to select a beneficiary or vary the amounts of the Trust. Step 2 - Does it pass the certainty of objects test: yes it is a complete list (if discretion, there is a discretionary Trust).

2. Is the class ascertain ability test concerned with conceptual or evidential uncertainty? Conceptual - must understand what the class means. Can you figure out who is who in the family? Next of kin- yes; Relatives – maybe; Friends/close friends – conceptually uncertain. Unless the beneficiaries are named, there is no need for a class, but if for example use the word to all "friends", to select close friends the Settlor could trust the Trustee to know who his friends are. In this case the Settlor or deceased relied on the Trustee to select the friends. If that Trustee dies first, a problem results as a new Trustee might not be able to do so.

Ask: could it be ascertainable by a complete list – yes. Evidentiary uncertainty - may have problems finding people fitting in the class. If this is the case, you can pay funds into court and have the court hear applications and decide.

Another Case - Testratrix left $10,000.00 to her "aged" housekeepers (in fact ages 21, 45, 87, 89). Is the Trust fixed or discretionary? At the time the Trust is created the objects must be certain - which ones are actually "aged"? The 89 year old? If age is not defined than there are possible problems. Try to make certain by the Testratrix's private definition and look at facts. Everything is relative to the people and circumstances. Therefore doesn't pass the certainty test unless a fixed Trust.

Another Example - If Objects are for all residents of Greater London (population: 10 million)

1. conceptually uncertain
2. evidentiary uncertain
3. administratively unworkable (capricious)

You would need in the Trust terms a Gift Over to cure the problem.

Termination of Trusts (Ending the Trust)

A Trust ends when the Trustees property is distributed in accordance with the terms of the Trust. There are several ways a Trust can be set aside – a Trust can end in other ways other than completion of the Trust terms:

1. Before completion: can have the power of revocation put in the terms of the Trust when completing the Trust terms.
2. The Trust is set aside: if the Settlor finds no power to revoke has been set out and if the Trust was made because of fraud, undue influence, duress, misrepresentation or mistake.
3. Termination by beneficiaries. If beneficiaries are *sui juris* (of adult age and sound mind) and have an absolute entitlement to all the interests. In order to defeat this, when making a Trust, have a Gift Over (i.e. to the unborn next of kin)

The purpose of this rule is to protect minors and to prevent control from " beyond the grave".

In some jurisdictions, there can be some variation if some of the beneficiaries are not of the age of majority and if they can show it is for the clear benefit of, or "more beneficial for, the underage beneficiaries. The court will grant an early vesting of the Trust.

Some Trust law enables a beneficiary to call for the distribution of Trust property contrary to the intention of the creator of the Trust. That is, a beneficiary is given a life interest in property and a general power of appointment over the capital, exercisable by deed or will, with a Gift Over, in default of appointment, to third parties.

APPENDIX A
A COMPUTER MODEL FOR CHOOSING AN OFFSHORE

This appendix concerns itself with the development of a computer model for choosing offshore tax havens. The objective is to develop a criteria for evaluating and choosing between tax havens. For those interested in specific statistics, the approach used is the inductive approach. This approach states that the conclusion is derived from the evidence. A more specific description of the problem would be to break it down into the following component pieces of information:

What information must be gathered? What factors must be considered? What weighting factor should be given to each characteristic? How can these factors be used to achieve the desired objective? The first statistical package analyses the data gathered from experts in the field of offshore tax haven. By utilizing the opinions of these experts, the first two component parts of the objective are satisfied. That is, to determine what information must be gathered, requires the general consensus of these experts on tax haven analysis. Who is more qualified to evaluate what information is to be gathered than those people who have proven their right to be considered an expert in the field. These experts were asked to choose those relevant factors that should be analyzed and to rate these factors in relation to their relative importance to the analysis. Certain additional factors were also suggested to these experts - the intention being to allow them the option of rejecting these by allocating a low weighting to their relative importance.

An option for additional suggestions that would aid the study was also inserted. This information was then combined and quantified in the statistical package for the total evaluation of all results obtained. The computer was programmed to do a regression analysis on the data and develop its weighting factors for the final solution of the problem.

The statistical model also produced statistics to determine whether or not a valid model could be developed. That is to say, whether or not the prescribed objective was feasible. If the resultant information showed a poor correlation, there would be very strong indications that a solution was not possible. Once the statistics were developed and analysed, they were used to develop a simulation model that would simulate the decision-making process for evaluating and choosing between tax havens. Finally, this evidence could be used to develop important results for present and future use in the analysis of offshore tax havens.

The previous chapters have discussed the elements involved in tax haven analysis. At this point in time, the characteristics, uses and entities specified need to be analysed in regard to statistical techniques to be able to develop a relationship between the elements involved. Once the guidelines for specifying a tax haven have been defined, we can distinguish between those countries that are to be considered in the analysis and those that are not to be considered. That is not to say, however, that those countries not considered as tax havens are not useful in international operations. This distinction in used merely as a guideline to narrow down the field of analysis to have a better understanding of the situation. With a narrower scope, a more concrete type of outcome can be derived and therefore utilised. The selection and definition of the entity used adds to the clarity of analysis. Thus, from the previous descriptions and definition a proper use of the statistical techniques will result in a more useful outcome.

This appendix is divided into five sections. The first section involves the choice of the statistical system to be used in the analysis. The statistical techniques discussed are regression analysis, multi-collinearity, the F statistic, the T statistic the level of confidence and a very brief analysis of others.

In choosing the statistical systems to be used for data analysis it was determined that many types of analysis were available, but only a selected few were possible. The data analysed required certain comparisons to develop a degree of relevance a characteristic had in relation to the required output. The data requires analysis of the interaction among the characteristics, as well as a total picture of the contribution of each element towards the finally validation. In addition, the interactive forces that might show one set of elements more relevant than another set is also important. The best combination of elements are also relevant. It should be noted that the second and third best indicators could be a better combination than the first and second in predicting the final output. This happens when several elements possess the same predictive values. For example, if one has a correlation of .7 and the other a correlation of .72, instead of the combination of the two being .85 or higher, the actual result in combination shows a correlation of only .72.

Another relevant comparison would be whether each of the above elements in combination was certain lesser ones will produce a better product and which one is the best combination. An element with a correlation appoints 72 can be combined within element of correlation of .4 and result in a correlation of .85 combined. Thus it is important that we look at the aggregate combination of groupings of characteristics rather than the individual correlation of each.

Other considerations besides these interactions all are, how reliable the data is and whether or not the output adheres to accepted confidence limits? Once these are determined, the data can be used to produce the desired simulation. Regression analysis was used, as it is the most popular and easily used approach to produce the best relationship between variables. An attempt was made to define or predict a mathematical equation that describes the variations among the variables analysed. A description of the scatter pattern of specific readings for each variable deviate from the resultant regression equation is required.

In regression we are defining an equation that is a reasonable fit to the scatter pattern of readings on each variable. If the equation fits within certain acceptable deviations, then it is said to fit the data and thus be used to derive relationships among the variables. Along with regression equation a correlation statistic is produced. This statistic measures the strength of the derived relationship. By extending the line or changing the variables, we can predict a dependent variable with a high level of certainty. The correlation measures the scatter of the readings about the predicted equation. The drawback in correlation analysis is it does not tell us whether .6 correlation is an acceptable level or not. It is up to other statistics to predict our confidence in the product or solution.

When one independent variable is a linear function of another independent variable or variables, it is referred to as perfect multicollinearity. The higher the collinearity, the more difficult it is to obtain a reasonable and unique solution. The regression coefficients are unbiased estimates of the population parameters, but multicollinearity creates a bias in the standard error of these coefficients. This widens the confidence interval thus reducing the reliability of the sample coefficients. Multicollinearity arises when some or all the independent variables are so highly interactive that it becomes impossible to disentangle influences on each other and thus obtain a reasonable estimate of their individual effects. In such a case a proper regression equation that is unique is impossible to obtain. Multicollinearity is a property of the sample data and not of the population. Therefore, it can be cured through adjustments that do not affect the corelative powers of the data.

The F statistic is used to test whether there are significant differences among the means of at least three samples. The F statistic looks at the ratio of the variance estimate based on the means in the sample over the variance in estimate from the actual individual readings in the sample. In such a test the null hypothesis would state that all observations are drawn from the same populations. If the null hypothesis is true then they have the same population and hopefully the same mean within certain reasonable limits. In other words, the null hypothesis states that the difference between the means in each observation is strictly due to sampling error.

The T statistic tells whether a sample is symmetric around a certain point. In this case, its value will be considered to be zero. The T distribution uses the concept called degrees of freedom in its measurement. These represent the number of linearly independent observations. The degree of freedom concept refers to the random selected observations minus any constraints on the data. One is deducted because the data used is from the sample of observations and not the total population. With the T distribution, such confidence or acceptance intervals can be constructed. To determine whether the mean values differ significantly from the normal mean we use the T statistic. If this statistic is within the established confidence level for the results on the linear relationship produced, we find that the means not differ significantly and therefore are acceptable.

The level of confidence is a term used when considering how accurate a sample is. Since these are random samples, we can only derive an answer in terms of a probability. As an alternative of valuation, we look at how likely we are to be wrong. That is, are we satisfied with 70 percent confidence or 90 percent or 100 percent? How much additional testing will it take to increase the confidence in our answer by another five percent? In using confidence limits, we are stating that the mean of the sample will come within the standard error limits (95 percent for example) of all possible samples. If we can derive this degree of confidence, we have a good idea of what to expect. The sample can also be related to the population. This implies that the following observations will be seen with increased sampling. If the sample sizes increased in size to that of the population, the same derived interval can be expected. The level of confidence provides more information whereby the smaller sample can be used in estimator or predictor of the total population.

Based on the analysis used in the previous section, it is a matter of choosing the sample reflecting the data to be analysed to produce a solution of how to choose a tax haven. The population to be sampled is a set of those people who give the advice to others on tax payments. Thus, using a small sample of advisers on tax havens, we can predict what the majority of all advisers would recommend. The ultimate result is that of a simulated direction for the decision process in choosing a tax haven. The bulk of advisers on tax havens are lawyers (approximately 70 percent) and accountants (approximately 25 percent). The names of advisers throughout the world were obtained from the publication list of various international tax haven magazines. The assumption being, that if you are a reader of these magazines, most likely you are also an adviser in the area. Once obtaining the names in the sample, it was found that this hypothesis was true.

Sampling Results

For the data analysed, the chosen confidence limit was 95 percent. It was felt that any greater probability than 95 percent would result in fruitless refining and wasted efforts to obtain the proper results. Increasing the expectation of accuracy five percent would not change any decisions based on the data obtained. The total number of people in the sample population was 10,000.

Ranking

With respect to the quality of data, it was necessary to develop a mechanism to rank the data given. To further refine the data, it is necessary to be able to rate the respondents experience. The more experience, the better the quality of data given. This was used as a guideline. The volume of international clients was also used as a guideline for determining competence of a consultant. The more time professional spends on giving tax haven advice, the better they are. To obtain such a ranking, all responses were asked to indicate how long they had been working on tax haven operations. The goal of the simulation process was not only to simulate the decision process, but to try to produce a better solution. The dominant characteristics found in the responses was the fact that although the ranking of characteristics was done properly, inconsistency was found in the choice of the best tax haven. The respondent was asked to name the best tax haven for each type of entity. An absence of consistency due to bias in the responded was encountered. Each respondent tended to use only one or two tax havens and really never considered the existence of others. Thus, they had created their own bias towards those that they had little knowledge off. The simulation overcomes such bias and produced a better solution. In any event, there was a startling consistency in the ratings.

The Program

The program developed for the analysis and choice of a tax haven involves a simplistic set of statements whereby built-in programs are used to perform all operational functions. The system was set up for the non-expert in computer programming who is more interested in the results than how it was obtained. The limitations, in this case, are the total dependence on the accuracy of the built-in functions that perform the required operations to provide the resultant statistics. One must have such confidence of the system to be able to adhere to the objectives of the research and not to digress from the main research idea. There must be a total confidence in the correctness and accuracy of all statistical functions used.

The program specified the variables to be used and feeds the uses for these into each of the functional sub programs. Each function has its own internal print mechanism. Therefore, an absence of external print operations exists. The program discussed is the final operating program used to produce statistics on data obtained about individuals using tax havens. It represents a comparison of only 13 variables that were derived due to prior elimination of those variables that were not considered significant in producing a solution. Programs are run to obtain statistics on three levels. These levels law are individuals, holding and trading companies, and Trusts. The main analysis was performed on individuals. Comparisons were run between the different levels to decide on similarities and differences. The following questions were asked at this stage in the programming:

Are the results from data obtained about individuals applicable to holding companies, trading companies and Trusts? Can conclusions obtained from the more comprehensive analysis on individuals be applied to the other levels? Do constraints in time and money warrant more analysis of these other levels?

Constraints

Based on the response rate and the number of variables to be analysed the maximum number of variables that can be used with any degree of efficiency was 14. Since 13 variables met the set of correlation of approximately .5, only 13 were used. To determine the correlation for comparison, two runs for each level were conducted. One run compared the first 5 while the other compared the last eight. The variables were also interchanged on the runs to determine if position affected the correlation. If the correlation for a variable had a radical change by significant mount, this analysis would have been abandoned. As it turned out, such was not the case. The correlation coefficient was used as a comparison guideline and from this the elimination was performed.

The holding company, trading company and Trust data needed a similar type of analysis as those given to the individuals. The question was whether or not more detailed analysis is required for these other entities? After running the analysis, it turned out that the final valuation differed only slightly when the entity was changed.

Adjustments were made for risk and other characteristics to determine the best predictive model. The data required more adjustments for usable results. The adjustments made were the introduction of a weighting factor on the raw data relating to experience dealing with tax havens. The questionnaire contained the valuation for ranking of time spent by the respondents in dealing with tax havens. Respondents tended to treat holding and trading companies exactly the same as Trusts.

Simulation and the Decision Process

With the development of the appropriate statistics, weighting factors and inferences it is now possible to be able to proceed towards the objective of developing a simulation of the decision-making process. The problem in the decision-making process by most professionals is that consultants do not operate on the premise of all available information. It is a basic tendency for consultants to utilise a limited amount of information and thus their options are actually limited in scope. With the use of the computer, this limitation in scope can be overcome and a better process can be developed. It is necessary to define certain terms of the use of the system. The simulation is defined as a dynamic representation that employs substitute elements to replace real or hypothetical components. The simulation represents a real situation, to provide a student or user with control over the situation and vary conditions during training, so that the task is made progressively more difficult.

The main objective in a simulation is that it is an attempt to identify the component's interactions that could occur in the process and duplicate what has been done. It is not an attempt to duplicate the outcome previously obtained, it is an attempt to duplicate processes used to develop the outcome. This transcends the limitation of the process and develops a better process. Using a simulation allows professionals and others to look at new situations in terms of the old model to predict outcomes in the future as well as identify any problems.

In making decisions on tax haven operations, the tax consultants will follow certain set of guidelines of operations that they developed over the years. This self-developed process is a result of accumulation of basic knowledge through following others more experienced in the field and possibly through their own practical education. The consultant builds up a fund of past experience through errors or work they have made in the past. The computer process isolates this past experience, identifies components and duplicates the process.

In general, such models can be broken into smaller operations that can be produced on individual basis without the use of the computer. When the smaller operations are combined, they form a set of operations that go beyond the capabilities of the single individual. Thus the simulation model will be developed to go beyond the current norm. The simulation model is a product of the person developing it. It therefore has a built-in constraint that corresponds to the limits and bias of its designer.

The concept used to in the determination of attributes and values is that of the prudent person. That is sound discretion is exercised by all parties concerned in the valuation and decision making. This discretion is based on the idea that one must observe how people of prudence, discretion and intelligence manage their own affairs. Care must be exercised by the consultant. Every prudent person can be expected to take risks, but they are based on sound judgement and a conservative outlook. We cannot build in the conditions where risk is taken on the basis of any emotional judgement. This cannot be programmed or predicted in the use of the computer model.

A rating scale must be set for the offshore tax haven, to show on a numerical basis, the difference between a characteristic that is poor or, average, good or even excellent. For example, the Bahamas would be designated as one that has an excellent communications system. It is important to determine how a broad subjective statement can be assigned a value within a numerical range, so it can be used in a computer model. The system used on the computer or in the model is designed to break down an attribute such as communication into its related components. If it can be broken down into enough components a relative rating scale can be used to develop and make accurate estimates of the level of all of the characteristics involved.

A communications system for a country involved in international operations requires speed and efficiency of lines from one country to another. The components would therefore be telegraph, telephone, Postal Service and fax for example. Each of these systems would be ranked according to the rating system of poor, average, good and excellent. These ratings would be assigned a numerical rating. The mid-numeric or range of these ratings would be assigned in accordance with factors for the type of communication component. For example, telegraph would be rated as 20 percent importance, telephone would be 25 percent, Postal Service would be 25 percent and fax would be rated at 30 percent. This is only an example. The total of all these factors would be 100. Reading each of these characteristics on a scale of one to a hundred multiplied by the weighting factor would give an absolute numerical value. To illustrate, assume a country had telephone with a rating of 25 percent. If it is given a poor rating of 25%, it is 25 percent multiplied by the weighting factor of 25 percent would give an absolute value of 6.75. Each characteristics would be multiplied in the similar manner and the four characteristics above for communication would be then added together to provide the rating for that country out of 100. This rating would then be used in the computer model as a decision making factor. All rating factors would be multiplied similarly and added into the formula in the computer to recognise other intangible weighting factors. This would determine the overall rating of that country for the particular client. Finally, the optimal ordering of comparison groups developed would be used to narrow the field of choice.

Thus the program is designed not to make a final choice, but to narrow the range of choices for that client. It would then be up to the adviser and the client to decide which one they prefer. The internal adjustment process inserted in the model adjusts for client preference and particular use. Those countries not within the scope of the client preferences would be eliminated from the choice factor before the valuation is done. In this way, if the client wanted a country in the Caribbean, this system would illuminate all non-Caribbean tax havens even if they had a higher rating. The goal of the system developed is not only to provide or decide which is the best tax haven, it is to decide which is the best tax haven in terms of the client preference.

A Simulation Approach

Generally, all simulations will involve a basic approach whereby certain relationships exist and are used. The first ingredient in the simulation process is to decide whether a tax haven should be used by the client. For example, if the client derives their income purely from domestic sources, there may not be an option to use tax havens. If their clients are not at a certain level of income, the cost of advice and constant update will be higher than the tax that they would pay under existing circumstances. This system will take the basic tax from the client's operation and relate them to the possible use of tax havens, in general. If the client cannot make use of any of the available prescribed uses, the program will reject the case immediately and print a message indicating "current laws do not facilitate the use of tax haven for this client".

The system will be a comparison whereby the uses are compared for the feasibility of their use. These attributes or combinations will be given quoted designations. The client's attributes are to be similarly coded and a scanner program will run a comparison for the minimum requirements. Each use will have these coded attributes and the computer can rapidly run the comparison. If any are usable, the computer will store this information and inform the adjustment mechanism that only the appropriate uses are available. In this way not only will the country be narrowed down, the uses would also be narrowed down. This would save a great deal in computer time in doing useless analysis. Any further restrictions will be coded into the system at this point and an automatic adjustment will make the necessary alterations.

Simulation 1

The first alternative system involves the use of a basic decision tree analysis. Each tax haven would be given a rating factor for each characteristic for the decision process. The computer mechanism would consider the most important variable first and progressively work down the list of variables. For example, if distance was the most important characteristic to be analyzed, then it would be considered first. A sub program is implemented to rate the list of tax payments for distance in relation to the clients home-based. A range would have to be set up so as not to eliminate all the choices at the beginning. From this comparison, all those offshore tax havens with a specific numerical rating would be taken and compared in relation to the next attribute. The next attribute would be, for example, tax treaties. It would either deal with countries containing tax treaties with the clients home country or we would specify to deal with the situation where they do not exist. The computer would then illuminate another group. At each stage, when the decision is made, a record would be kept of those countries that were eliminated. Finally, when enough comparison are performed, several offshore tax havens will result. Possible uses of these offshore tax havens will then be disclosed along with the countries chosen as best prospects.

Simulation 2

This approach is similar to the first, in that it uses a step-by-step illumination. The difference being that the elimination process is only carried out for several variables. The step-by-step elimination process is only carried out for the first three variables to reduce the choice to five or six. At this stage, comparisons would cease and a new analysis would be initialised. The new analysis is a rating game for those tax havens that are left. This scheme would rate each haven on a scale for each of the remaining variables. The top five havens would then be chosen. These would be the five for the highest numerical score. The final five would then be listed with a general description of all characteristics as well as possible uses that were developed earlier. It would then be up to the user to decide which they prefer of those remaining.

Simulation 3

The last simulation would be to implement a relative rating scheme with weighted factors for all the offshore tax havens keeping in mind the special features of the client involved. Each haven would be given a numerical score for each variable to be analysed. The individual statistics would then be weighed in relation to importance and clients co-operation. The previously specified alternatives could be modified to eliminate immediate disadvantages. It is important to develop a good base to work from.

The Simulation Program

Once the simulation approach is decided upon and the characteristics are determined, it would be beneficial to look at what the program on the computer would look like. Prior or to analysing the program, the constraints that must be added or allowed are reviewed. One can only expect to be able to use a limited set of available information. The longer the research., the more information can be gathered. Gathering of information about countries is highly costly and time-consuming.

The researcher can never compile all information about all countries and uses and be totally up-to-date. Tax laws are changing and each country added makes the system more complicated. Thus there must be a cut-off as to when the researcher for the program should stop gathering new information and the decision is to be made.

Another constraint is limited computer access and funds available for access. Any basic computer operation has a basic limit as far as its use is concerned. Use is also limited by the power of the computer involved. This limitation changes over the years as computers are becoming more and more powerful and the size of memory is also increasing.

The final constraint, is the restriction on the number of uses that could be picked up for use in the simulation (note that could be more constraints that might impact the system). To be able to produce the uses available for a scheme would require the communication of a group of professionals located in the countries involved. This is a highly costly exercise. One could not expect to cover everything. With a change in Location there will be adjustments required and new systems or elimination of old ones. The model must include a constant update facility to be successful.

The Program and its Workings

The program is made up of a main program and five sub-routines (subs). Each sub is designed to cover a specific function. The following discussion of each segment includes a detail description of its working as well as the elements to be used in the specified functions. The benefit of using a modular approach for designing such a program is that as new concepts are found to impact the decision-making process, a sub-routine can be added to account for that new concept. Also, as certain concepts become out of date, a sub-routine can be fully eliminated with minor adjustments to the main program. Thus the modular approach allows more flexibility in decide on the components of the program where conditions are constantly changing over time. The sub-routines used in this simulation are:

1. Sub-routine "Can Use"
2. Sub-routine "Prefer"
3. Sub-routine "Gather"
4. Sub-routine "Choose"
5. Sub-routine "Compare".

The names of the sub-routines are a good indication of what they do. Sub-routine "Can Use" tests to see if the client can use offshore tax havens. Sub-routine "Prefer" adds the elements of a client's preference. Sub-routine "Gather" gathers information about specific offshore tax havens. Sub-routine "Choose" chooses an attribute to be compared. Sub-routine "Compare" compares the attributes for the havens, then illuminates those not within specific guidelines. The main program ties all the sub-routines together. At the various stages of operation, control can always return to main program. This feature provides for the instances where certain restrictions are not there. For example, if an applied operation is evaluated for cost savings. If this test fails, control revert to a special area where a client is informed that it is not a cost benefit in considering offshore tax havens as an alternative.

Another example of return of control to the main program occurs with sub-routine Can Uses. This program looks at the uses of tax havens. If there are no uses available to the client, it is not feasible to set up an offshore tax haven operation. The computer uses a counter to record the uses available. When the sub-routine is made all its comparisons, and the counter still has a positive value, control returns to the main program where the next test is made. Under these circumstances, all other steps are limited to data regarding the status of that client and its use of offshore tax havens.

The system as it stands, provides a solid base for the development of offshore tax haven use. It tests mainly the important characteristics as well as analyses client operations for the use of havens. At each stage, control can be put in to ensure continued smooth operation of the system in relation to the changing nature of a business. Remaining discussion relate to a more detail description of the actual programming involved, the key to the system and the full logic.

The Sub-routine Can Use

This sub flows operates through three main loops. A counter is set up and nested functions perform comparisons and a resultant printout of available uses. The parameters needed to be retained are from the main program as follows: the clients characteristics are designated in the array named "client", a counter is set up for the number of uses and one is set up for the number of characteristics in the client's operation.

The problem encountered is that all uses will require different characteristics. Many uses require the existence of 6 characteristics while others require 7,8 or 9. In addition, some characteristics are absolutely necessary, while others are not necessary but are desirable. A further modification in the system will be to set up another set of loops to test other minor requirements. This modification makes the sub extremely complicated, requiring an increase in computer time and difficulty to adjust for problems.

The first statements analysed involve the main loops for the nesting operation. This loop is the first one encountered and last one to be exited from. The other loops can all be contained within this main set of statements. A counter is used in the loop to keep track of the number of matching characteristics encountered. The counter is set to zero each time and new uses fed into the system. Therefore, the use of the counter is used exclusively for analysis of the individual characteristics of each use. Before any commands are to be given, the system needs a test to search for the end of the list. This ensures there will be no problems of the computer running to infinity.

The next loop asks the computer to do the designated comparisons. The loop is flexible in that it will only operate as many comparisons as there are characteristics in a particular use. The next loop compares the various use characteristics, as presented in the loop, to each of the included characteristics of the client. This determines if the characteristics exist in the clients operation. The testing statements indicates the following: if the client characteristics match with those of the uses of offshore tax havens, control is transferred to another statement and the counter is increased to show the match has resulted. The computer is then commanded to print a coded message to the client. Once a use is available, the computer could be automatically programmed to hold the details of the match in its memory banks for a later printout. When all the characteristics are compared, and a favourable response is not obtained, the last loop transfers control back to the second loop. At this time another characteristic is brought into the comparison. If there are no more characteristics to be compared then the program is finished.

Sub-routine Prefer

This sub-routine was put into the program to allow greater flexibility through adjustment of the program to client preference. Although it is very small, it represents a routine with powerful service value. The client is paying the fee and it is the objective of the system to be able to make recommendations to clients. If the system is designed to alter itself in accordance with preferences of the client, the service provided is more professional and therefore more useful. This sub-routine is placed in the program to prove that such a feature is possible. The preference allowed for, in this case, is that of a choice of geographical area. This is only a test.

The sub-routine can also handle more than 1 preference at a time. By using these preferences, certain tax havens can be eliminated as choices. This is done by use of the binary system in marking a code beside those particular tax havens that are no longer available for comparative purposes. The program has the capability of cater-ing to client preference regarding uses, country, and weighting factors for characteristics they feel or more important than others. In most professional and client relations, it is usually the consultant who decides the order of importance of the characteristics, this system allows for the possibility that the client might want to add restrictions . As can be seen, if the client has other advisers, the system can adjust for their preferences as well. This sub-routine adds a great deal of flexibility to the program proposed.

Sub-routine Gather

Sub-routine "Gather" acts as a controlling system for all the information evaluated in the remaining sub-routines. As its name indi-cates, it's main function is to gather information produced in other sub-routines. The sub-routine provides added flexibility to the system. If the system needs to be modified with more sub-routines added, it pro-vides an avenue for modification without upsetting the main program in all it workings. The sub-routine compiles the information of previ-ous functions and utilises sub-routines "Choose" and "Compare" to perform the remaining comparison operations in evaluating which off-shore tax havens should be chosen and used in the final analysis. The main information gathered from previous the fact that tax havens can be used, what uses are available and any preference the client might have regarding particular offshore tax havens. Sub-routine "Gather" reads the attribute ratings for each of the remaining offshore tax havens after adjustments have been made for the previously men-tioned client preferences. It then calls the other sub-routines used to choose an attribute for comparison purposes.

Keeping each function in a separate sub-routine also simplifies an already complex system. As the system is improved and modified, it becomes more complicated. If a choice at any stage in the program needs to be repeated at another time, all that is required is one statement with a specification of apparent parameters required to be compared. Control is then transferred back to the sub-routine. Sub-routine "Choose" then calls sub-routine "Compare" to run the required comparisons and limitations after an attribute has been chosen. Once all the attributes have been chosen control returns to sub-routine "Gather" for the final adjustments and printing of the final product. At various stages, tests are made to see whether more comparisons need be made and whether a final result has been attained.

Sub-routine "Gather" is fed information from the main program through its parameters. The parameter in each offshore tax haven is reserved for results obtained in the next sub-routines. If any parameter has a code of zero, the interpretation is that the haven designated is not to be used in any of the subsequent comparisons. Each component will have the proper numerical code to be able to determine which haven is being considered.

More specifically, the first sub-routine reads in the rating factors for each of the attributes for the offshore tax havens in question. These ratings are on a scale of 1 to 99. The value zero is eliminated as it adds confusion and numerical problems to the weighted comparisons that will be made. The value 100 is eliminated as a space saver, that is it requires a third digit for storage. The premise being, the difference between 99 and 100 is not material enough to change any decisions. Each routine for each offshore tax haven will have one such number assigned to it for comparison and elimination purposes. A counter is set to zero at this point. This counter will be used to check whether the number of havens left for comparison purposes is greater than the specified minimum, which in this case is 5. Once that minimum of 5 is reached, more comparisons will not be required. The first loop encountered sets the counter equal to the number of tax havens to be compared. The loop then goes through all the offshore tax havens, if a non-naught number is encountered, the counter is increased by one. If a special code is encountered in any of the codes the computer is instructed to look at the next base in the array without any increase in the counter. After the loop is completed, the counter should have a value equal to number of non-zero spaces in the array. Once all the comparisons have been made, the computer is instructed to move outside of the array and continue with the program.

Sub-routines "Choose" is then called to perform the remaining comparisons and limitations. Information in the counter and the array is transferred to this sub-routine. This sub-routine then calls sub-routine "Compare" to establish its limitations. The counter will be reduced in the sub-routines until it has a value of 5 or less. Control then returns to sub-routine "Gather" as the objective of the sub-routines will have been obtained.

The next loop goes through the array T from sub-routine "Choose" and stores the non-zero components in location H. Therefore, the total can only contain a non-zero positive numerical value for further comparison. The next loop in the sub-routine takes the remaining offshore tax havens and multiplies them by the appropriate weighting factor as determined in the statistical analysis or by client preferences. The rating is then printed for the client to be able to choose which they think is best. The loop or array continues its work until the number on the counter equals the number of remaining offshore tax havens to be considered. If the counter is equal to zero or 1, the steps in the loop will be performed once and control is transferred out of the loop. The program also includes a test for a zero value.

Sub-routine Choose

Sub-routines "Choose" is designed to choose an attribute in order of importance or according to client preference. This attribute is then compared for all the offshore tax havens remaining after an elimination process to produce a list of offshore tax havens available. The ordering of steps in this sub-routine is very important. The use of ordering significantly reduces all memory requirements, number of statements and run-time. When all comparisons are completed, control is transferred back to sub-routine "Gather". The use of a discrete ordering in the sub-routine has the ultimate benefit of elimination of wasted space and time. Each time a comparison is made, control will be transferred to sub-routine "Compare" to make the comparison and then control returns back to sub-routine "Choose" to continue with its steps. At each stage in the process, a comparison is made to ensure that we have not gone below the minimum requirement (which in this case is five). Once five tax havens are left, control is returned to the main program.

Sub-routine Compare

The objective of sub-routine compare is to run a comparison of the ratings of each offshore tax haven for a particular attribute. This comparison will distinguish between the better quality offshore tax havens unless there is a preference by the client in question. The use of a separate sub-routine is described earlier. It reduces the required memory space and number of statements. When sub-routine "Compare" is called, the variables read in and the counter will be used to ensure that the limit of five is upheld. The array T will be used to eliminate those offshore tax havens that do not fall within the pre-scribed guidelines. The array character is used to read in the values for all offshore tax havens for the particular attribute being tested. Once a routine is used the counter is terminated. This allows its value to be changed for each new character being tested. The value is set to zero and memory is cleared. This space would be used to store the maxim rating for a particular attribute. This rating is to be used as a basis for comparison. The first loop will determine what the maxim rating is and subsequent runs through the loop will adjust its value. This loop goes through all the offshore tax havens tested to make sure we're not taking a maxim for the tax haven that is not acceptable for comparison purposes. Once all havens are probed, the value in the memory location "great" will be set as the maximum. The next loop reduces the value of "great" by 30 points. In this way, if the offshore tax haven has a rating greater than or equal to the value in the loca-tion "great", it will be within 30 per points of the maximum rating. The next array does a comparison of the remaining offshore tax havens. In this way, the remaining non-zero havens are tested and adjusted. When this is completed, control returns to sub-routine "Choose" for the next case or termination of the testing.

Main Program

The main program tests the client's data to determine whether the cost of offshore advice is greater than the benefit that might arise. If the cost is justified, then sub-routine "Can Use" is referred to; this tests for the available uses of offshore tax havens that are available to the client. Control returns to the main program and a test is made to determine which specific uses they can actually use if any. If none are available, control goes to a coded message in the program. If a use is available, the data is adjusted in accordance with client preferences through sub-routine "Prefer". Once "Prefer" is finished, control reverts to the main program that reads the ratings for all the havens and calls "Gather" to perform its operations as described previously. Finally, the rating for the simulation is completed. The main program, is used to control all the functions of the computer system. This approach allows for the maximum flexibility to be maintained.

Outcome and Results

The goal of the simulation model was to simulate the decision processes of consultants giving advice on offshore tax havens. Analysing the input data, the expected outcome produces a model that would duplicate the decision-making process. This would indicate to the client which offshore tax haven is best for their needs and how it should be used. The product of the simulation was to be a distinct choice of the offshore tax haven and its best use. Certain ideas could be formulated based on the main characteristics involved and a better model could be developed. Outside consultant make a decision based on limited data and therefore choose those uses and countries that they feel our most appropriate based on their limited knowledge. The weakness in this approach is that the choices are being made based on what the consultant has knowledge of or in many cases, the easiest for the consultant. This choice is not necessarily the best for the client. The advantage of the computer simulation is that it is not limited to the knowledge of one individual.

APPENDIX B
MORE INTERNATIONAL LAW

Article 18 (Vienna Convention on the Law of Treaties)

This is the test used by the court. There is an obligation not to defeat the object and purpose of a treaty prior to its entry into force. So, if you signed a treaty, not yet in force, are there obligations under International Law: (note that you are not bound under Article 18 to carry out the treaty) but you must refrain from acts that will defeat the object and purpose of the treaty:

1. where ratified and not in force yet
2. where signed, but not ratified.

   Article 18(a) – signed the treaty, constituting the treaty subject to ratification - only until you make intention clear – not to become a party to the Treaty- you are not going to ratify, or

   Article 18(b) – where you have ratified the treaty but it is not in force and the entry 'into force' of the treaty is not unduly delayed (problems here with the meaning). The Vienna Convention , for example was open for signature in 1969 and not effective until 1980.

Example Re: Article 18 - object and purpose: the law of the Sea Treaty opened for signatures in 1982 and was not in effect until

1994. Historically, 10-20 years is normal. The obligations under Article 18 don't exist in custom and Article 18 may represent custom, it may not, but probably not customary when adopted, but it is now. Example would be if 2 countries enter into an agreement, and both ratify, but it is not in force. One country does something that defeats the object and purpose, i.e. Mexico and Ecuador sign a treaty prohibiting hunting and protecting the habitat of pink flamingos and Ecuador does nothing - and hunters still hunt and breeding grounds are not cleaned up and Mexico has issued a bounty of pink flamingos because they are destroying crops.

Reservations on a Treaty

To what extent and in what circumstances can you enter a reservation to a treaty and what are the effects as between you and the other states?

1. permissibility of reservations – do you allow them?
2. opposability – to what extent are your relationships affected with other states (this is not a problem with a bilateral treaty – with 2 states, but will be with more states and multi-lateral treaties)

Why would you want to allow reservations at all? The policy aspect: unless every party agreed- there would be no reservations practice under the League of Nations: you must have reservations if you want significant number of states to sign the treaty. There are some treaties, however that can not have reservations like a peace treaty, or any constituent treaty that acts as a Charter. The treaty will say whether or not it is open to reservations. (i.e. The Law of the Sea treaty - 1982: there were some provisions that were open to reservations. Typically a procedural thing – less so in substantive norms). The moral force of having widespread adherence. The more numbers you get, the greater likelihood of evidence of custom.

Federal states will enter a reservation, but only with in the power to carry out a treaty. The same with Canada and jurisdiction issues between the federal government and provinces. Federal states will enter a reservation, but only within the power to carry out the treaty. Same with Canada – with jurisdiction issues between the federal government and the provinces. Some treaties allow reservations on specific parts – some are silent (i.e. the Genocide Convention, 1951) - would you want to allow a reservation to a convention on genocide.

Permissibility and Oppose Ability

It is possible to make a reservation so long as it is not incompatible with the objects and purpose of the treaty and the reserving state is regarded as a party to the convention. Compatibility is the test: the state enters a reservation to a multi-lateral treaty and if another state objects (another contracting party) to what it considers to be incompatible with the object and purpose of the convention, can consider the reserving state to not be a party to the convention.
Effects:

1. not allowing the state to become part of the treaty
2. allowing with qualifications.

The practice under the League of Nations: the reserving state could not become part of the treaty. Every state had a veto power. Does this work? When there is a greater diversity of interest and emphasis on moral significance. The court held the Rule is not appropriate and too strict.

The test for opposability: to countries that have been bound. Consequences for opposing a treaty:

1. can be part of the treaty even with a reservation , or
2. state owes no obligation to other state (i.e. Ecuador to Mexico Re: flamingos)

Test: if they regard the reservation as being incompatible with the object and purpose of treaty therefore the Object and purpose defines permissibility and opposability, i.e. If Mexico says it does not oppose the treaty, but makes a reservation, a state can refuse to be a part of the treaty or modify a version of the treaty anytime. Mexico will not be bound by a unilateral modification.

The court is ambiguous – if a state opposes a reservation – they can consider that state as a non-party, even if incompatible, they could still consider them a party. The test for permissibility makes sense, but opposability is ambiguous.

Article 20(4)(b): unless a contrary objection is Expressed, the treaty comes into force. Objecting to a reservation not because of incompatibility, but because you don't like it- so it comes into force - except for the reservation.

Effects: distinction between a state objecting to a reservation, but does not oppose coming into force.

Result: modifies the treaty to the extent of the reservation.

The effects of reservation on a state that does not object:

The objecting state: must specify within a specific time period, the provision doesn't exist, and the treaty is in force, except for the reservation, and accept the reservation (its legal effect).

Article 21 (1): modifies for both the reserving and the accepting state, the provisions of the treaty - this is a reciprocal modification.

The Legal Effect of Treaties

Article 26 (Vienna Convention): treaty obligations have to be honoured.

Article 34: Treaty does not create rights and obligations for a third state without its consent.

Treaty and internal law conflict: (i.e. Canada enters into a treaty prohibiting land mine production and a Canadian engineer discovers a way to make land mines and allows him to produce them. If someone objects (i.e. Sweden), which law prevails? Canada's domestic law or treaty obligations?

Article 27 – depends upon the tribunal - if international law applies, you can not plead domestic law as an excuse for a breach or a justification for breach. There would be a different result in Canadian court Re: international law in a domestic court. Exception (Article 46): possibility of invalid treaties - where internal law can be looked at narrowly and never successfully pleaded. Article 27 notes Article 46.

Article 46: when a treaty is entered into in violation of internal law with respect to competence to conclude the treaty- it is usually constitutional. Provisions of internal law regarding competence to conclude treaties. There are limited means of avoiding obligations when conclusion of a treaty was done in violation of fundamental law where that requirement was manifestly evident. It does not talk about power to implement, only conclude.

1. violation must be manifest – the world is on notice (blatant)
2. internal law must be of fundamental importance.

Example: Peru has a provision in the constitution requiring advise and consent of the Senate plus the signature of the President before a treaty can be ratified. Under a ?majority, the Senate agreed so the President signed. The subsequent election of a new President disavows the treaty. This is not a breach of international law because everyone knew the treaty was entered in violation.

A Canadian example: Canada entered a Treaty on a labour conventions case: they signed and ratified it, but the province of Alberta objects saying it is a matter within provincial jurisdiction, not federal. The court held *ultra vires* the federal government when it is the responsibility of the provinces and the legislation was struck down. The federal government can not comply with the treaty obligations. Issue: is Canada in breach of international law – or can it plead Article 46?

- is it manifest?
- the law has nothing to do with Canada's ability on the treaty, it just can't implement them

- Canada ends up in breach of international law
- Canada's competence to enter in Treaty rests with the Federal government
- this provision comes up rarely

Operation of Treaties

A nation can only invalidate consent to a treaty if:

1. an error (Article 43)
2. there is fraud in the treaty making (Articles 48,49, 50)
3. reservations (Article 50)
4. there is coercion in the treaty making process (Article 52); if coercion it is voidable , if...procured by threat or force, it is void

Example: Annexation of Czechoslovakia in 1939 by the Germans - the Czech President reportedly was chased around a table and they held his hand and forced his signature. This was a basis for voiding the treaty.

Articles 53, 64, 71: *Jus Cogens* – the pre-emptory norms of international law that can not be contracted out of. The norm now recognised by the world, as being one from which no derogation is possible/permitted. The statement of fact- some norms of international law that you can not escape even in treaty obligations, i.e. slavery - suppose Sudan were to enter a treaty with Libya and Libya agrees to return fleeing slaves - that treaty is void as impermissible.

- can contract out of customary law but not *jus cogens*
- if a new *jus cogens* evolves, any existing treaty in violation becomes void
- use of treatment by force, genocide, piracy, slavery, racial discrimination (apartheid), terrorism, hostage-taking
- evolving norms may include nuclear weapons - not clearly a violation of a norm - maybe gender oriented crimes or environmental issues may arise.

Example: threat, use of force (other than in self-defence), and genocide are impermissible and that state can not enter a valid treaty with another state. The matter is within the international community who has a generalised interest.

Qualification: you can invalidate a treaty because of a fundamental change in circumstances

Article 62: *Rebus sic stantibus* (has never been pleaded successfully) - there are two elements

1. provision in the treaty must go to the core- the bargain has to be at the core of the provision. The change in circumstance can't be incidental, but be essential for gaining consent.
2. the effect of the change in circumstances must radically change the nature of the obligations under the treaty (analogous to frustration). The basis of the agreement has just exploded, i.e. the treaty of socialist friendship between the Soviet Union and the Eastern Republics - a collapse of socialism – is the basis of treaty disappearance.

Custom

General Customary Law is different from protocol:

- the norm of custom: that you don't arrest diplomats is custom
- that a dean of a diplomatic corporation gets to shake hands first at a reception is protocol

Test: consistent practice among nations - do they believe it is law? As a matter of law you do not do number 1 above, or the state would be in breach of number 2.

Article 38 Vienna Convention on the Law of Treaties: rules in a treaty becoming binding on third states through international custom.

Test: general practice + belief (*opinio juris*) = law. It is not law until it is recognised as law, therefore *opinio juris*. At some point, they must have engaged in a practice without the belief you are bound, therefore the concept has problems with the requirements. Practice must be a belief of the requirement to be legally bound.

Law identification: parallel unilateralism - states just start doing things and assert claims – the other states start doing it also and over time the general practice becomes law – which is the *opinio juris* doctrine:

Example: the Continental Shelf, which is now law. In 1945, when the US discovered oil in the gulf, they asserted legal rights to the minerals on the Continental Shelf - the states did not object and other states began asserting rights also. By the mid-1950s the Continental Shelf was a doctrine of international law.

Opinio juris – describes whether or not International law exists (used by the international court)

General Issues Regarding Custom

What states are entitled to make custom (universal assent of states) can't bind sovereigns whether or not consent. Is it enough to acquiescence?

Do some states get more weight than others? Example: the US has the same weight as Switzerland in the law of the Sea - true essentially, but in practice?

When does the practice take place - more recent practice or a century ago - timing of the practice?

What if the states object to custom - can you have a rule that doesn't bind (i.e. Norway had a 4-mile zone when everyone else had a 3-mile zone). States will generally follow *opinio juris;* belief in an engaged practice as norm of customary international law - will state typically say it is refraining from some act because it is bound to by law? No, norm is that you are doing it *ex gratio,* as a nice state, not because you are bound. Courts can infer *opinio juris* from the nature of the practice, although they are not willing to do so universally.

Does customary law just apply to some states (argue the principles of regional national law, i.e. in Russia, helping other socialist states, or a sub-net of states).

Rules of Treaties in Proof of Custom (as set out in the North Sea Continental Shelf Case)

- direct effect on the parties to the treaty
- may be used because they are practical and legally binding (strong evidence) as proof of custom
- a norm in a treaty may also exist in custom and a norm may exist before a treaty (codification of international law)

Step 1: Ask who is a party to the treaty? A treaty is not in effect with a country if they signed it but had not ratified it.

Step 2: Is it a codification exercise?

Step 3: Determine if it is a codification

- Treaty led to custom
- Treaty and subsequent practice led to custom

The Geneva Convention was a bargaining exercise. To determine:

How customary law emerges :

Take for example the EEZ (Exclusive Economic Zone) – a state can not enter a reservation Re: this. Only a bargain Re: a 200-mile zone, and before the convention came into force is customary international law created. The treaty negotiation was in process. Re: the North Sea the court held that where you can't negotiate but you can be "equidistant", though this is vague. The convention allows for reservations, but not true for Article 1, which declares the existence of customary international law. Therefore the nature of circumstances show that the parties were not contemplating customary law.

At best this law is evolving and not a black letter law. The treaty with subsequent practice can have an impact that creates customary international law (i.e. a series of bilateral treaties with a common element and this can be used as indicative of custom such as diplomatic relations - customary law in existence – is an indicia to prove it existed. Look to a series of bilateral treaties that can be used as evidence).

The subsequent practice: the states ratified. States using principle of equidistant when negotiating the continental shelf therefore it is now a customary norm. The "Lotus Rational": even if generality of practice doesn't necessarily prove custom because you haven't proved *opinio juris*. The court also deals with the nature of general practice – is it satisfied with the practice (not long enough time here)

When the court looks at practice they review the following:

1. duration of practice (the convention was only in force for five years)
2. look at raw numbers - numbers of states engaged in the practice and how widespread is the practice

Which states have the issue at the core? How do you weight the practice of different states so that everyone is equal (i.e. the states with a small Continental Shelf). Therefore the court looks at the practice of the states which have the most interest. Nine maritime states with the strongest interest in shipping or coastal states with a significant interest in offshore or that need to protect their coast were considered (i.e. US, Canada – coastal, Greece – maritime). Interests often will conflict, even within a country (i.e. US) with two distinct interests. The result is that some states appear to count more than others therefore the factors must be balanced.

Rule: Customary international law binds a state for good. States can not change their mind later, even if the government changes. Objections must be original (as custom is developing) and if they are silent, this equals consent; they must do something. So, as an example, if Saudi Arabia objects, then the court says they are not bound by custom.

This is:

- a question of fact
- a question of circumstances

Final Principle: The Calvo Clauses. In the Latin American constitutions, a clause was put in with a constitutional requirement for investment agreements between the host state and foreign investors. The clause stated that any disagreements between the host state and investor state must be dealt with within the host state country and they were restricted to the legal requirements of the host state – the matter couldn't go for diplomatic help (i.e. call in the US Marines). This used to be a Latin American norm. Peru recognised this and saw it as binding, but Britain saw their own right in a conflict to protect the investor. Therefore there was a clash between international and regional custom, i.e. Latin America gives clause effect and US refuses to give effect (right to protect an individual is the right of a sovereign and cannot be waived by a private citizen – regional norm directed at non-regional parties).

ENDNOTES

[1]Sigler, J.D., Burritt, H.C. and Stinnett, S.E. (August 1996) "Cyberspace: The Final Frontier For International Tax Concepts?", *Journal of International Taxation*, p. 340.

[2]*Ibid.*, p. 341.

[3]Multi-product suppliers are service providers who pay for various products from business and other concerns. It has been stated that there was already hundreds of millions of Internet users by the turn of the century. Access to the Internet is provided by a system of these service providers. They offer (for a fee, although competition may soon do away with provider fees entirely) access to the Internet and specialised access to many products such as billboards of information and connections to libraries and other sources of information. Such information is not localised to that of a particular country, it ranges from information from sites across North America, Europe, Australia, etc.

[4]*Supra* note 1, p. 341.

[5]See "A Selected Tax Policy: Implications of Global Electronic Commerce", Department of the Treasury, Office of Tax Policy, November 1996. See also the report on the Internet at www.ustreas.gov, and the Clinton Administration Paper of July 1997 "A Framework for Global Electronic Commerce" which can be found at the Web site www.white-house.gov

[6]The authors of the treasury discussion paper have emphasised that it is not to be considered a white paper. Their intent is to identify and assess some of the issues.

[7]"Electronic Commerce Opportunities and Challenge for Government", *OECD* 1997. A report by the Australian Tax Office is "Tax and the Internet", August 1997, available on the Internet at www.ato.gov.au; Revenue Canada's Advisory Committee on Electronic Commerce were represented at the OECD conference on electronic commerce in November 1997 in Turku, Finland.

[8]*Ibid.* Authorities in Canada and Australia have guardedly expressed the view that there needs to be some form of consistency of treatment for transactions on the Internet and similar transactions completed through another medium (i.e. telephone, telex, fax or even personal contact).

[9]Ormrod, C.T. (19th November 1997) "Income Tax Issues Arising Out Of Electronic Commerce", *Canadian Tax Foundation*, 49th Annual Conference, p. 6.

[10]An example from Canadian legislation would be the definition in the *Income Tax Act*, R.S.C. 1985, c.1 (5th Supp.), as amended (hereinafter referred to as the Act). Unless otherwise stated statutory references are to the Act. Subsection 248(1) of the Act defines *person* as "any word or expression descriptive of a person, includes any corporation, and any entity exempt..." The importance is that it includes corporations and others as well as individuals.

[11]Shareware is software developed by individuals and companies and offered on the Internet. In the past it has been offered free to anyone who has access. For example, when Microsoft Windows95 came out, there was a problem with several printers made by Canon and their ability to print through Windows95. The problem resulted in the last page of every print job or a part thereof being omitted. Canon offered on its Web site a downloadable program that would solve the problem and the service was free and offered to everyone. Some types of shareware have a minimal charge attached to them and others are making a small profit.

[12]*Supra* note 10.

[13]*Consumers Software Inc.* v. *R.* [1995] 2 C.T.C. 2851 (T.C.C.).

[14]*Ibid.*

[15]"Changes to Withholding Rates Under the Revised Protocol to the Canada-US Convention" (1994) *Conference Report,* Report of Proceedings of the Forty-sixth Tax Conference, July 1995 (Toronto: Canadian Tax Foundation), 2:91-103.

[16]Article 4(2) of the Convention between the Government of Canada and the Government of Japan for the Avoidance of Double Taxation and the

Prevention of Fiscal Evasion with respect to taxes on Income, signed at Tokyo on 7th May 7 1986.

[17]In the 1993 budget, Finance Minister Don Mazankowski announced the intention eliminate withholding tax in its negotiations of bilateral tax treaties.

[18]Convention between Canada and the US with respect to Taxes on Income and on Capital, signed on 26th September 1980 as amended by the protocols, signed on 14th June 1983, 28th March 1984, and 17th March 1995, Article V, paragraph 1. See Article VII(1) of the Protocol.

[19]*Ibid.* Article VII(2) of the Protocol.

[20]See the United States, Treasury Department, "Technical Explanation of the Convention", 26th April 1984.

[21]See Canada, Department of Finance *Release*, no.94-076, 31st August 1994.

[22]If a Canadian resident makes a royalty payment to a resident of a third country in respect of property located physically in the US, the US-Canada Tax Convention deems the payment to arise in the US.

[23]Most US income tax treaties provide a definition of royalties under Article 12(2) of the US Model Tax Convention. The treaty defines a royalty as payments of any kind received as consideration for the use of, or right to use, any copyright of literary, artistic, or scientific work, any patent, trademark, design or model, plan, secret formula or process, or other like property, or for information concerning industrial, commercial, or scientific experience. Some treaties also include payments for technical assistance, know-how, or "show how" as a royalty, if the assistance is ancillary to another royalty generating right.

[24]*Supra* note 1, p. 346.

[25]*Supra* note 9, p. 11.

[26]Section 253 of the Act.

[27]See *Interpretation Bulletin*, It-420R3 for Revenue Canada's view of the application of this definition and their elaboration on the computation of income subject to tax.

[28]*L. Hollinger* v. *MNR* [1972] CTC 592, at 600 (FCTO), see also *Canadian Marconi Company* v. *The Queen* [1986] 2 CTC 465, and *Esg Holdings Ltd.* v. *The Queen* [1976] CTC 295.

[29]*Supra* note 9, p. 14.

[30]*Ibid.,* p. 17.

[31]*Ibid.*

[32]*Quebec Pharmaceutical Association* v. *T. Eaton Co. Ltd.*, 56 CCC 172.

[33]*London Life Insurance Co.* v. *The Queen*, [1990] CTC 43.

[34]Kyres, C.A. (1995) "Carrying on Business in Canada", vol.43, no.5, *Canadian Tax Journal,* pp. 1629-1671.

[35]Section 253 of the Act.

[36]*Sudden Valley Inc.* v. *The Queen*, 76 DTC 6178 (FCTD).

[37]*Supra* note 9, p. 23.

[38]The 1992 Organisation for Economic Co-operation and Development (OECD) Model Income Tax Convention on Income and Capital, updated as of 1st September 1995.

[39]Paragraphs 1,3 and 4 of Article 5 of the 1992 OECD Model Tax Convention list the following as indicating the presence or absence of a permanent establishment:

Establishes a PE / a place of management, branch, office, factory, workshop, or mine, well, quarry or other place for the extraction of natural resources; *Is Not a PE* / use of facilities solely for the purpose of storage, display, or delivery of goods or merchandise; the maintenance of inventory solely for purposes of storage, display or delivery; the presence of inventory solely for the purposes of being purchased by another enterprise; a fixed place of business solely for the purpose of purchasing goods or merchandise, or of collecting information; a fixed place of business solely for carrying on preparatory or auxiliary activities.

[40]Article 5(4) of the OECD Model Tax Convention, see also article 5(4) of the US Model Income Tax Convention of 16th June 1981.

[41]The Code contains a limited definition of *trade or business within the US*. This definition does not properly address the problem of Cyberspace.

All cases not governed by Subsection 864 (b) are left to the courts and the IRS to decide. This is not the most desirable situation as there is too much uncertainty of outcome.

[42]The US common law has several cases where the problem might arise. See *De Amodio* 34 DTC 894 (1960), and *Spermacet Whaling & Shipping Co.* S/A, 281 F.2d 646 (CA-6, 1960).

[43]*Supra* note 18. Article V, paragraph 1.

[44]*Supra* note 9 at 17.

[45]Paragraph 5 of the Commentary on Article 5 of the Update of the OECD Model Tax Convention, approved 22nd October 1997.

[46]Article VII of the Canada-US Income Tax Convention.

[47]*Supra* note 1, p. 341.

[48]*Supra* note 9, p. 12. Subsection 2(3) of the Act.

[49]Durnford, J. (1991) "The Distinction between income from Business and Income from Property, and the Concept of Carrying On Business", *Canadian Tax Journal, vol. 39, Number 5.*

[50]Revenue Canada Roundtable (1994) *1993 Conference Report, Report of the Proceedings of the Forty-fifth Tax Conference* (Toronto: Canadian Tax Foundation) 58:15-16.

[51]Brown, C.A. (1994) "The Canadian Income Tax Treatment of Computer Software Payments", vol.42, no.3, *Canadian Tax Journal 593-613*, or Murray, K.J, (1993) "Computer Software: Canadian and Cross-Border Issues", *Ibid.*, p. 27:1.

[52]See the 13th September 1994 letter from the Reorganisations and Foreign Division of Revenue Canada in Revenue Canada Views, document no. 9319685. Note that Canada's treaty with the Netherlands exempts such payments from withholding tax.

[53]*Supra* note 1, p. 342.

[54]OECD (1992) "The Tax Treatment of Software", reprinted in *Issues in International Taxation No.4*, Model Tax Convention: Four Related Studies 74.

[55]US LTR RUL 9128025. The payments in respect of the license of computer software were considered copyright royalties.

[56]US LTR RUL 9231002. This contrary to the treatment mentioned in LTR RUL 9128025. The ruling goes further to limit the application of this ruling by stating "...we conclude that taxpayer's...contracts involve a '*sale* or *disposition*' within the meaning of section 1.451-5(a) of the regulations. At the same time...payments received under taxpayer's...contracts may in fact, constitute 'Royalties'".

[57]*Wodehouse*, 337 US 369 (1949), see also *Misbourne Pictures et al.* v. *James W. Johnson*, 189 F.2d 774 (CA- 2, 1951).

[58]*Supra* note 11. Some examples are games and programs developed by internal programmers of software and hardware companies during their spare time. These range from software to make calendars to those that are computer games that could not be marketed or had no marketing value.

[59]*Supra* note 1, p. 344.

[60]*Supra* note 1, p. 345.

[61]Paragraph 862(a)(4) of the US Code.

[62]OECD (12th June 1997) *Electronic Commerce Opportunities and Challenges for Government*, Paris: OECD.

[63]Revenue Canada (10th April 1997) *Backgrounder*, Ottawa: Advisory Committee on Electronic Commerce.

[64]Australian Taxation Office, *Electronic Commerce Project- Terms of Reference, #1*. The complete terms can be found at the Web site www.ato.au.

[65]Australian Taxation Office, *Supporting the Community - Plan for 1997-2000*, available on the Internet at www.ato.gov.au.

[66]*Supra* note 5.

[67]See 1st July 1997 Press Release "Response to Today's White House Release of 'Framework for Global Electronic Commerce' statements by Fort Wayne Mayor Paul Helmke, President, The US Conference of Mayors". This can be found on their Web site at www.usmayors.org.

68*Supra* note 5. The report goes into a detailed analysis of these issues. It is enough to know that these are similar issues to those being discussed by many countries.

69Paragraph 18(1)(a) of the Act.

70"Revenue Canada Round Table" (1993) *Report of the Proceedings of the Forty-fourth Tax Conference,* 1992 Conference Report, Toronto: Canadian Tax Foundation, 54:1-75, question 11, p. 54:8.

71*Window on Canadian Tax*, Don Mills, Ontario: CCH Canadian, par. 2118.

72Revenue Canada (16th February 1990) *Interpretation Bulletin It-283R2*, par. 14.

73See the Canada-United States Free Trade Agreement Implementation Act, SC 1988, c.65, Section 61, amending Section 2 of the Copyright Act, RSC 1985, c.C-42.

74Cohen, B. (1997) "Selected Tax Policy Implications of Global Electronic Commerce", *Report of Proceedings of the Forty-eighth Tax Conference*, 1996 Conference Report, Toronto: Canadian Tax Foundation, 38:1-19.

75One need only look to the major changes in the larger North American banking/financial institutions to see the validity of this notion. There have been major mergers, and talk of proposed mergers, in both the US and Canada. The rationale has been competition on a global scale.

INDEX